JESUS
AS PORTRAYED IN
THE NEW TESTAMENT

Books by Michael Fallon

All published by
Chevalier Press,
1 Roma Avenue,
Kensington NSW 2033
(02) 9662 7894

A Companion to the Catechism of the Catholic Church, 2013
Introduction to the Old Testament, 2014
Praying the Psalms with Jesus 2018

Introductory Commentaries on the Bible

The Gospel according to Saint Matthew 1997^1, 2005^2, 2018^3
The Gospel according to Saint Mark 1997^1, 2009^2
The Gospel according to Saint Luke 1997^1, 2007^2
The Gospel according to Saint John 1998^1, 2005^2, 2016^3
The Acts of the Apostles, 2003
New Testament Letters Volume 1 Paul, 2004
New Testament Letters Volume 2 James, Peter, Hebrews, Jude & John, 2004
The Apocalypse: a call to embrace the Love that is stronger than death, 2002
Genesis, 2008
A Priestly Kingdom and a Holy Nation: Exodus, Leviticus and Numbers, 2008
Deuteronomy, Joshua, Judges, 2008
Isaiah, 2009
Israel's Eighth Century Prophets: Amos, Hosea, Isaiah, Micah, 2011
Israel's Seventh Century Prophets: Zephaniah, Nahum, Habakkuk, Jeremiah, 2011
Israel's Sixth Century Prophets: Ezekiel, Isaiah 40-55; Haggai, Zechariah, Isaiah 56-66, 2011
Israel's Fifth Century Prophets: Obadiah, Zechariah 9-14, Joel, Malachi, Jonah (& Daniel), 2011
The Psalms 2005
Israel's Festival Scrolls: Song of Songs, Ruth, Lamentations, Ecclesiastes, Esther, 2011
Proverbs & Job, 2011
First and Second Samuel & First Chronicles, 2012
First and Second Kings & Second Chronicles, 2012
Ezra & Nehemiah, 2012
First and Second Maccabees, 2012
Tobit & Judith, 2012
Wisdom of Ben Sira & Wisdom of Solomon, 2012

Published 2017 on my website: mbfallon.com

The Christian New Testament and the Islamic Qur'an: a comparison

JESUS
AS PORTRAYED IN THE NEW TESTAMENT

DIVINE LOVE IN A HUMAN HEART

MICHAEL FALLON MSC

COVENTRY
PRESS

Published in Australia by
Coventry Press
33 Scoresby Road
Bayswater Vic. 3153
Australia

ISBN 9780648861225

Copyright © Michael Fallon 2020

All rights reserved. Other than for the purposes and subject to the conditions prescribed under the *Copyright Act*, no part of this publication may be reproduced, stored in a retrieval system, or transmitted in any form or by any means, electronic, mechanical, photocopying, recording or otherwise, without the prior permission of the publisher.

Scripture quotations are from the author.

Nihil obstat:	Reverend Gerard Diamond MA (Oxon), LSS, D.Theol
Imprimatur:	Very Reverend Joseph Caddy AM Lic.Soc.Sci VG Vicar General Archdiocese of Melbourne
Date:	01 June 2020

The Nihil Obstat and Imprimatur are official declarations that a book or pamphlet is free of doctrinal or moral error. No implication is contained therein that those who have granted the Nihil Obstat and Imprimatur agree with the contents, opinions or statements expressed. They do not necessarily signify that the work is approved as a basic text for catechetical instruction.

Cataloguing-in-Publication entry is available from the National Library of Australia http:/catalogue.nla.gov.au/.

Cover design by Ian James - www.jgd.com.au
Cover image: painting by Michael J Nelson "Jesus kneeling in prayer and meditation" Used by permission.
Text design by Megan Low (Film Shot Graphics - FSG)
Text set in Source Serif Pro

Printed in Australia

CONTENTS

Preface 7
Chapter One   'God' 9
Chapter Two   Jesus' Contemporaries and their
                     Image of God 27
Chapter Three   Jesus' Image of God 47
Chapter Four   Jesus' Communion with God 59
Chapter Five   Jesus' Love 65
Chapter Six   Jesus the Word of God Made Flesh . 81
Chapter Seven   Jesus' Teaching about our
                     Response to God................ 87
Chapter Eight   Jesus' Conception.............. 105
Chapter Nine   Jesus' Miracles 111
Chapter Ten   Jesus Died as he Lived 139
Chapter Eleven   Jesus the Crucified One who Lives . 155
Chapter Twelve   Jesus the Saviour of the World.... 185
Chapter Thirteen   So, Who is Jesus? 199

PREFACE

The story of any people reveals a pervading fascination with things divine. We are no exception. Some try to build walls round the city of the human spirit, but the divine cannot be kept out; it is within, at the heart of our being. Our questions cannot be suppressed, any more than our experiences can be denied.

One such question is 'Who is God?' It is a very practical question, really, for on its answer depends the way we live our lives in the light of our religious experiences. It arises when we take seriously the mystery of our living and our loving. Granted the depth of the question and the limits of our minds, it is not surprising that answers differ. The tragedy is not that our answers differ, but that they so often share an undertone of fear, arising from the insecurity that is part of the human condition.

It is here that the subject of this book becomes significant. As we shall see, those who knew Jesus of Nazareth saw in him the answer to this ultimate question. When they asked 'Who is God?', they came to point to Jesus, for they saw in him the human expression (the incarnation) of God. They also observed in him a way of living that revealed to them how someone free from fear of God or other people could respond to the divine.

It is hard to keep impressions sharp and clear, and we have an uncanny ability not only to forget but also to distort. The historical Jesus, too, has been distorted in many ways through the centuries, with the consequence that often the

Jesus presented by Christians has failed to connect with people's life-questions. Christians have even been guilty of oppression in his name.

Yet Jesus was not an idea; he was a person who lived and died in this world of ours. Fortunately we have in the New Testament the record of the impression he made on those who grew to love him. With disciplined study, it is possible to clarify the essential features of this wonderful person, and so to correct many of the false portraits that abound. Saints and scholars will be forever refining our insights into this rich material but, while there will always be areas of debate, the New Testament – as I hope this book will show – is not unclear in its portrayal of Jesus.

I have been living with the question for many years, and wish to share with the reader what I have come to see, so that together we can come to know the real Jesus of Nazareth. The answer can be found only when we share our lives in love, and take time to relish and deepen our experiences in prayer. Studying the texts can act as a stimulus, inviting us to this personal encounter. It can also guide us through the shoals of self-deception.

I hope that we can all come to know Jesus more truly, and that, listening to the desires of his heart, we may be more effective and more courageous in continuing his healing mission of love in this very lovable and very love-needy world.

Feast of Saints Peter and Paul, 29 June 2020

CHAPTER ONE

'GOD'

In seeking to know Jesus we will be speaking a lot about 'God'. What are we referring to when we speak of 'God'? What was Jesus referring to when he spoke of, and prayed to, 'God'?

Knowing

We know something when the judgment we make about it is in accordance with the way it is. We experience something through our senses, or we experience a feeling, an emotion, a thought or desire in our inner world. We know what we experience in the outer or inner world when we focus on it, and when our inquiry into our experience leads to insight, an insight that stands up to scrutiny. The first thing we must state is that God is not among the objects that we experience in either our outer or our inner world.

In the New Testament the Beloved Disciple expresses this truth when he states: 'no one has ever seen God' (John 1:18; see 1John 4:12). Likewise Paul: 'No one has ever seen or can see God' (1 Timothy 6:16). They are stating a fundamental truth that they found in their tradition. There is a story in the Book of Exodus (33:18ff) in which Moses is portrayed as pleading to see God. God tells him that it is not possible: 'You cannot see my face' (Exodus 33:23). God assures Moses that he will pass close to him. God covers Moses' face and removes the cover only after God has passed by. Moses has to be content with seeing what the writer calls God's 'back'. That is to say, Moses has to be content with the Torah, which shows the path we must follow to be in communion with the mysterious God whom we cannot see.

Since we do not experience God, we do not know God in the sense that we can form a certain judgment about God that is based on insight into experience.

Believing

We don't have the time or the skill to check everything for ourselves. In every field of learning, a person has their contribution to make, but we would scarcely make any progress in any field without believing the results of other peoples' work. We can be mistaken and may have to adjust, but progress in knowledge requires belief. However, when it comes to God, everyone suffers from the same limitations: we cannot experience God. No one can. So we cannot believe in God based on the fact that other people experience and know God, and we believe them. No one can experience God. So no one can know God based on experience.

Sometimes, we choose to believe because others believe. We trust them because of the quality of their lives and the good that flows from their belief. It is here that we must look when we speak of belief in God. We choose to believe in God because others whom we trust believe in God, and because their belief, while going beyond what we know, does not contradict it. We choose to believe in God because we see that their lives are richer because of their belief. We choose to continue to believe because we find that our lives are enriched by this belief.

As Christians we believe in God because Jesus believed in God. Jesus is our 'leader in faith' (Hebrews 12:2). As Paul writes: 'I live by the faith of the Son of God, loving me and giving himself for me' (Galatians 2:20).

The concept of God

In every act of experiencing, two things are happening. There is the experiencing of the object, and there is at the same time a consciousness of myself as the one experiencing. This is true when our focus is on something outside. It is also true when we reflect back and focus on ourselves. Consciousness of the self is an essential dimension of any act of experiencing.

Let us look first at the objects that we experience. None of them has within itself sufficient grounds for the fact that it exists. Everything we experience depends on something outside itself to account for its existence. Nothing would exist if there did not exist a non-dependent Reality that has within itself all that is needed to exist. It is this Reality that is the sustaining cause of everything that exists. We call this Reality 'God', 'in whom we live and move and have our being' (Acts 17:28).

A study of religions shows that people have sensed that there is this creating and sustaining presence in their lives, and have associated it with the 'spirit' of a grove of trees, or a spring, or a mountain, or fire, or thunder and lightning, or the sun, or the moon, or the star-studded heavens. Others associate this Reality with an event in their history. For the Israelites, it was the Exodus from Egypt.

The time came when people came to think that there is only one ultimate Reality: that the sacred presence somehow intuited in myself is the same presence intuited in the grove of trees and in the spring, and in the words that come to us through special people who touch our hearts and confirm our sense of ourselves. People came to experience everything as connected, as belonging, as held in existence by one and the same sustaining Presence, one and the same 'God'. People came to see the whole cosmos as an explosion of God's Self-giving, and as expressing something of God.

This is reinforced when we focus on our consciousness. We experience objects *as* we are. Is it not true, for example, that when we are loved we seek differently, we focus differently, we see differently? It is reasonable from the fact that we are conscious of ourselves as loved to infer that there must be someone loving us. Similarly with the consciousness of receiving life as a gift, and the consciousness of being called, and being inspired, and led. We speak of such experiences as mystical. To a greater or lesser extent, everyone is conscious of having such experiences. We infer from this that there must be someone loving me, gifting me with life, calling, inspiring and sending me, and we call that someone 'God'.

The history of religions witnesses to the myriad ways in which peoples have built up a concept of God. It is here that Jesus of Nazareth has a special importance. Being human, Jesus could not experience God, but he was conscious of himself as deeply loved, and he shared the way he conceived God as Love. Impressed as they were by Jesus, his disciples grew to share Jesus' faith and, impressed by the quality of the lives lived by believers, people down through the centuries have wanted to believe in the God Jesus believed in, and they have continued to believe because of the way this belief has enhanced their lives. This belief has been the contribution of the Christian community to the world.

A key conclusion from the above is that when we use words to speak of God, we must do so only with the most profound humility. We must begin with the realisation that no words can comprehensively express a Reality that transcends our necessarily limited experience. We must begin also with the conviction that everyone has a contribution to make here: every culture, every thinker, every artist, every lover.

Believing as Jesus of Nazareth believed

For the moment, let us simply recall that Jesus lived a beautiful life, and that he saw his life as an expression of his communion with God. This is something that those who knew him well came to see. As one of us, he shows what a human being is capable of when we live out our communion with God. Because he did this, he revealed something wonderful about God.

The history of religion demonstrates how we project onto God our hopes, our desires, our fears, and our prejudices. Jesus cleared a way through all this. His disciples came to believe that God, the mysterious Presence that holds us in existence, is Love (1 John 4:16). Well, that is the best word that Jesus' disciples could come up with to speak of God as revealed by Jesus. They came to see that the universe is God's Self-gift. Everything is an expression of this Love. No wonder we look for love, and seek to know more so that we can be in deeper communion. We do not experience God as an object, but we do experience ourselves as receiving existence and as loved. When we choose to 'be-lieve' this (when we choose to 'be' in this 'love' that sustains us in existence), we believe in God as Jesus believed in God, and we live in gratitude to Jesus who showed us this amazing truth: that God, the sustaining source of everything, is Love.

Believing in Jesus includes a commitment to get to know Jesus better, to listen to his words and watch his way of relating to people. He believed in God as Love; and his disciples came to believe that everything Jesus was and everything he said and did flowed from the intimate communion he experienced with the One whom he and his contemporaries called God.

Relating to God is fundamentally and necessarily an experience of myself, the knowing subject, as receiving existence, and as being loved and inspired. When we pause to enjoy communing with nature (the grove of trees, the spring, or a mountain, or the moon), we sense a sacred presence that draws us to the heart of nature, and at the same time mysteriously transcends what we are experiencing. This is especially so in a loving relationship. We find ourselves, to some degree, in communion with God.

Jesus wants us to share in his experience of being loved, and in the God who he believed was loving and inspiring him. Jesus drew people into this experience, an experience that was already happening in the core of their being, but they did not dare to believe it till he encouraged them by the example of his love. For Jesus, God is the source of all he is. God is self-giving love. No wonder Jesus was open to everyone. No wonder he believed in people. He knew that he was loved, and he knew that this was true for everyone. We don't have to change our lives to be loved by God. Of course, we want to change our lives, for we want to 'live and live to the full' (John 10:10). But this is not a pre-requisite for being loved by God. Quite the contrary, it is God's love that offers us the grace to change, if we would only believe in God's love and welcome it.

If by the word 'God' we mean the God that Jesus revealed, we have to make space in our lives to reflect on what we really long for. We want to belong. We want to be at home in the universe. We want to be in communion with God, which is to say communion with the sacred mystery that is at the heart of everything and everyone. God is what we all share, and we all belong to each other. We are one with the universe. Everything is a radiance of God. Jesus believed this. Any God who is less than this is not yet truly the God who sustains us in existence. Every creature yearns for communion with this God.

Jesus' religious heritage believed that the whole of creation is an expression of God's 'Word', an expression of God's will to share God's Being. This is expressed beautifully in the biblical drama where we hear God say: 'Let there be light' (Genesis 1:3). When, out of his communion with God, a prophet spoke, this too was received as an expression of God's 'Word', God's Self-revelation. The Prologue of the Gospel of the Beloved Disciple reaches its climax when he declares: 'The Word was made flesh and dwelt among us' (John 1:14). He is speaking of Jesus. The Genesis account speaks of human beings as created by God to be 'in God's image and likeness' (Genesis 1:26). Here in Jesus, at last in the history of the human race, is a man who is completely open to God's grace, completely open to welcome the love he experienced and to let it bear fruit in his relationships with people.

He experienced the weakness, the fragility that is part of what it is to be human (this is what the word 'flesh' expresses), but, as the Letter to the Hebrews states, while he was like us in everything (including all that is expressed in the word 'flesh'), 'he did not sin' (Hebrews 4:15). That is to say, he never said No to love, he kept trusting his experience of being loved (even while he experienced being crucified). This is how he revealed that God is love.

Jesus and God

The New Testament uses the word 'God' nearly twelve hundred times. The reference is to the One Jesus believed in, prayed to, and spoke of, the God he called by the affectionate word 'Abba', the God he revealed in all he was, in all he said and did. In the man Jesus, God is manifesting God's presence. When, before knowing Jesus, the disciples had sought an answer to the question 'Who is God?' they had looked to the Exodus event and seen God revealed as a liberator and saviour, as the God of faithful, covenant love. Now, having come to know Jesus, and having experienced a new covenant of love and a new liberation and fullness of life, they looked to Jesus to reveal God. They came to believe that 'God in Christ was reconciling the world to God' (2 Corinthians 5:19).

To answer the question 'Who is God?', Jesus' disciples learned to contemplate Jesus. To answer the question 'Who is Jesus?', they learned to look upon him as the presence and revelation of the God in whom he and they believed. They saw this in everything Jesus was, in everything he did and said. It was especially and finally seen on the cross: 'When you have lifted up the Son of Man, then you will know that I am' (John 8:28). 'I am' translates the Greek *ego eimi*, which translates a Hebrew expression that is linked to *YHWH*, the 'name' revealed to Moses at the burning bush (Exodus 3:15). Jesus revealed the One he addressed as Father (Abba) as the redeemer God. It was from the cross that Jesus' disciples experienced the power of Jesus' life-giving Spirit in their lives.

Matthew captures something of this in his final portrait in which he presents the exalted Jesus in glory on a mountain in Galilee. The Risen Jesus authoritatively commissions the Eleven to carry on his mission of bringing about the reign of

God. He promises them in words that speak of the presence and power of God: 'Know that I am with you always; yes, to the end of time' (Matthew 28:20). These words are an echo of the promise made to Joseph at Jesus' conception: 'They will call him Immanuel, a name which means God-is-with-us' (Matthew 1:23).

Jesus spoke of God. Jesus prayed to God. His disciples shared his belief because of the quality of Jesus' life, and the fruit of believing that they experienced in their own lives. By the end of the first century, we find the Christian community embracing the practice of including Jesus when they spoke of 'God'. We find this in a letter written in the opening years of the second century to the Christian community in Ephesus: 'Our God, even Jesus the Messiah, was borne in the womb by Mary according to the dispensation of God, of the seed of David and of the Holy Spirit' (Ignatius, the bishop of Antioch, Ephesians 18). In his letter to the Christian community in Rome, Ignatius writes: 'Suffer me to copy the passion of my God' (Romans, 6). It is possible that an example of this practice is found in the Prologue to John's Gospel, composed in the last decade of the first century. Some early manuscripts read: 'No one has ever seen God. It is the only Son, who is in the bosom of the Father, who has made God known' (John 1:18). Other manuscripts include the word 'God' in speaking of Jesus: 'It is *God* the only Son'.

The early Christians lived in a world that associated the word 'God' with a range of objects, including the emperor. Christians wanted to include Jesus, of course in a way that is consistent with strict monotheism. What set the Christian use of the word 'God' apart from its use by every other group was that Jesus' disciples believed that to speak of God we must keep our eyes on Jesus. For them it is Jesus who reveals the one true God. This practice also witnesses to the fact that they were not content to admire Jesus while failing to listen to or watch God being revealed in and through him. The essence of Christianity is that in listening to Jesus and watching him, and in experiencing something of the intimacy of his prayer, we are truly being drawn into communion with God.

When we Christians say that Jesus is God, or say that Mary is the mother of God, we are not claiming that Jesus is another God. Jesus is a man, but in such an extraordinary purity that it is God, the one God in whom Jews and Christians believe, who is revealed in and through him.

Up to this point, we have used the word 'know' to refer to a judgment of fact based on discernment of experience (see page 5). In Biblical language, the word 'know' can refer to the experience that comes from communion in love. Using the word 'know' in this most intimate sense, Jesus assured his disciples: 'If you knew me you would know my Father also' (John 8:19). 'The Father knows me and I know the Father' (John 10:14-15). 'if you see me you are seeing the Father' (John 14:9). 'The Father and I are one' (John 10:30).

Christians came to speak of Jesus as having two natures. The word 'nature' is a scientific term born of observation. We come to know something's nature by observing what it does. When his disciples watched Jesus and listened to him, his human nature was obvious. He showed them what we human beings can be at our best. But they came to see more than this: they came to believe that what Jesus was saying and doing was revealing God, insofar as God can be revealed in a human being. That is Jesus' divine nature. He invites everyone to share this nature with him. In his Second Letter, Peter prays that his readers 'may become participants of the divine nature' (2 Peter 1:4). Jesus wants us to share the intimate communion that he has with the one he believed is God, so that we, too, will speak God's words and be instruments to each other of God's life-giving love.

Jesus' followers were amazed at the purity and beauty of Jesus' love. Through Jesus' teaching and actions, they came to believe that God, the one God who is the source of all and who holds everything and everyone in existence, is Self-bestowing Love. They believed that the human Jesus was totally caught up in this divine love. It is God who heals through Jesus. It is God who loves through him. Jesus and the God he called 'Father' are one in a complete communion. It is their mutual love that is spoken of as the 'Holy Spirit'. Jesus believed that it was God's will that he share this Spirit of love with his disciples, and ultimately with every person on earth.

It was largely their experience of sharing in this love that explains the growth of Christian communities, and that attracted people to find in the Christian community a way of life that satisfied their search for meaning. As Paul wrote in his Letter to the Christian community in Rome: 'Hope does not disappoint us, because God's love has been poured into our hearts through the Holy Spirit that has been given to us' (Romans 5:5). And to the community in Philippi he wrote: 'If there is any appeal in the Messiah, any consolation from love, any communion in the Spirit, any movements of compassion and feelings of love, make my joy complete: be of the same mind, having the same love, being of one soul and one mind ... Let the same mind be in you that was in the Messiah Jesus' (Philippians 2:1-2, 5).

We cannot see the Transcendent God, but we believe that in watching Jesus we are watching how God reveals God's Self in a human being. The whole of creation is a 'word' of God. Jesus is the human expression (the 'incarnation') of God, and so reveals God in a human way. Jesus says: 'If you know me, you will know my Father also. Whoever sees me has seen the Father' (John 14:7, 9). When we speak of God's 'Word', we are speaking of God achieving God's will through creating and embracing in love. We Christians see Jesus as expressing this Word in a fully beautiful human way. We believe that this One God is constantly active in history, and Jesus helps us to see and feel what this loving presence and action is like. He enables us to find human words to direct us to better ways of thinking of God. He is a constant corrective to our tendency to misunderstand God by projecting onto God our limited concepts and dysfunctional habits of thinking.

The whole of creation exists because it is a finite participation in the very being of God. Everything is an expression (a limited, imperfect, but real expression) of God. Everything belongs, because everything is held in existence by, and gives expression to, the One God. This was Jesus' belief, and we are invited to share it. Never is our teaching concerning God intended to compromise Jesus' belief and our belief in the truth we share with our Jewish and Muslim brothers and sisters and others that there is one God. Seeing Jesus as the Word of God in human form reminds us to listen to all the ways God speaks to us. Watching Jesus inspired by God reminds us to wonder at the way God pours God's life-giving Spirit into each of us, embracing us in love and drawing us into communion with God. The God revealed by Jesus is a God of all-embracing, all-encompassing Love. Jesus' disciples began by getting to know Jesus. It was obvious that he was human like them, but there was something quite special about him: his healing love. Gradually they came to see that this amazing love came from his special communion with God whom he called 'Abba'. Knowing (in the biblical sense) God as 'Father', Jesus knew himself as God's 'Son'.

The Gospel of the Beloved Disciple witnesses to the fact that misunderstanding the nature of the relationship between Jesus and God was already a factor in the debates of the last decade of the first century when the Gospel was composed. It is evident that Jews who did not accept Jesus as the promised Messiah (this group is called 'the Jews' throughout the Gospel) were debating with the Jews who accepted Jesus as the Messiah.

In John chapter 5, we find an account of Jesus healing a man. Because the healing took place on the Sabbath, we are told: 'The Jews started persecuting Jesus, because he was doing such things on the Sabbath' (John 5:16). We are then given Jesus' response: 'My Father is still working, and I also am working' (John 5:17). The text continues: 'For this reason the Jews were seeking all the more to kill him, because he was not only breaking the Sabbath, but was also calling God his own Father, thereby making himself equal to God' (John 5:18). That this is not how the Beloved Disciple understood Jesus' claim is clear from Jesus' response: 'Jesus said to them: Very truly, I tell you, the Son can do nothing on his own, but only what he sees the Father doing; for whatever the Father does, the Son does likewise. The Father loves the Son and shows him all that the Father is doing' (John 5:19-20).

When Jesus speaks of God, he is speaking of his experience of being unconditionally loved. The Beloved Disciple expresses this beautifully in his Prologue: 'No one has ever seen God. It is the only Son, who is in the bosom of the Father, who has made God known' (John 1:18). Jesus puts it this way: 'The Father knows me, and I know the Father ... The Father loves me' (John 10:15, 17).

The Beloved Disciple in his Gospel constantly focuses on Jesus' communion with God: 'The one who comes from heaven (from communion with God in prayer) testifies to what he has seen and heard' (John 3:31-32). 'The one who is from God has "seen" the Father' (John 6:46). Jesus experienced himself as on a mission given him by God: 'The living Father has sent me, and I live because of the Father' (John 6:57). 'I know the Father because I am from the Father and it is the Father who sent me' (John 7:29).

Jesus' words flow from his communion with God. 'He whom God has sent speaks God's words, for he gives the Spirit without measure' (John 3:34). 'My teaching is not mine but the Father who sent me. Anyone who resolves to do the will of God will know whether the teaching is from God or whether I am speaking on my own' (John 7:16-17). 'I declare to the world what I have learned from God ... I speak these things as the Father instructed me' (John 8:26, 28). 'I declare what I have "seen" in my Father's presence' (John 8:38). 'I know God, and I keep God's word' (John 8:55). 'Do you not believe that I am in the Father and the Father is in me? The words I say to you I do not speak as from myself' (John 14:10). 'The word that you hear is not mine. It is from the Father who sent me' (John 14:24). In a prayer to God, Jesus says: 'The words that you gave me I have given to them, and they have received them and know in truth that I came from you; and they have believed that you sent me' (John 17:8).

Jesus' words come from his prayer. So do his actions: 'My food is to do the will of the One who sent me and to complete God's work' (John 4:34). 'The Son can do nothing on his own, but only what he sees the Father doing. For whatever the Father does, the Son does likewise. The Father loves the Son and shows him all that the Father is doing' (John 5:19-20). 'I have come from heaven (from his intimate communion with God), not to do my own will, but the will of the One who sent me' (John 6:38). 'I can do nothing on my own. As I hear, I judge; and my judgment is just, because I seek to do not my own will but the will of the One who sent me' (John 5:30). 'The deeds that the Father has given me to complete, the very deeds that I am doing, testify on my behalf that the Father has sent me' (John 5:36).

Jesus said, 'When you have lifted up the Son of Man, then you will realise that I AM, and that I do nothing on my own. The Father who sent me is with me and has not left me alone, for I always do what is pleasing to my Father' (John 8:28-29).'It is the Father living in me who is doing this work' (John 14:10). Jesus prays: 'I glorified you on earth by finishing the work that you gave me to do' (John 17:4). 'Jesus cried aloud: Whoever believes in me believes not in me but in the One who sent me. And whoever sees me sees the One who sent me. I have come as light into the world, so that everyone who believes in me should not remain in the darkness' (John 12:44-46).

It was from his intimate communion with God that Jesus experienced the call and the grace to share with others the revelation that he received from God: 'I do nothing on my own, but I speak these things as the Father instructed me. And the one who sent me is with me. The Father has not left me alone, for I always do what is pleasing to my Father' (John 8:28-29). 'I declare to the world what I have heard from my Father' (John 8:26). 'I declare what I have seen in the Father's presence' (John 8:38).

My aim in quoting from the Gospel of the Beloved Disciple is to state that neither Jesus nor his followers thought of Jesus as another God who claimed equality with God. On the contrary, Jesus acknowledged that everything he is comes from God, as do his words and actions. 'Jesus said to them, "My food is to do the will of the One who sent me and to complete my Father's work' (John 4:34). 'I can do nothing on my own. As I hear, I judge; and my judgment is just, because I seek to do not my own will but the will of the One who sent me' (John 5:30). 'The deeds that the Father has given me to complete, the very deeds that I am doing, testify on my behalf that the Father has sent me' (John 5:36). 'I do nothing on my own. It is the Father living in me who is doing this work' (John 14:10). 'Jesus cried aloud: Whoever believes in me believes not in me but in the One who sent me. And whoever sees me sees the One who sent me' (John 12:44-45).

Jesus is like us in everything except sin. Being human like us, he did not, he could not, experience God as an object. He was conscious of himself as being loved, and, drawing on the tradition in which he was nurtured, he interpreted the experience as coming from the one he was brought up to call 'God'. When he declares that his whole desire was to do God's will, there was nothing blind or unthinking about his obedience. The word 'obedient' means listening (Latin *audiens*) and from close union (Latin *ob*). Jesus had to apply all his heart and soul and mind and strength to discern how best to respond to the love he experienced. He did this so beautifully and faithfully that his disciples attempted to follow his example and to live in the same Spirit. This is the essence of Christianity.

Jesus' disciples came to see him as the perfect human expression (the 'incarnation') of God. When we speak of Jesus' divinity, we are speaking of his intimate communion with God: 'I am not alone; the Father is with me' (John 16:32). Not everyone listened: 'You are trying to kill me, a man who told you the truth that I heard from God' (John 8:40). Such was the intimacy of this communion that Jesus could say:

'The Father and I are one' (John 10:30). Here again, 'the Jews' misunderstood his claim: 'The Jews took up stones again to stone him. Jesus replied, "I have shown you many good works from the Father. For which of these are you going to stone me?" The Jews answered, 'It is not for a good work that we are going to stone you, but for blasphemy, because you, though only a human being, are making yourself God' (John 10:31-33). Jesus was never 'making himself God'. Nor were his disciples. Jesus' claim, and the claim of Christians, is that Jesus is 'God's Son' (John 10:36). He enjoyed such intimate communion with God that he could say: 'The Father is in me and I am in the Father' (John 10:38).

The Spirit of God filled his heart, his prayer, his life. Jesus revealed God in the love that flowed from this communion, a love, as noted earlier, that gave authority to his words, and healing and liberating power to his relationships. And Jesus wants everyone to experience this communion: 'The Spirit abides in you, and will be in you' (John 15:17). 'You will know that I am in my Father, and you in me, and I in you' (John 14:20). 'My Father will love you, and we will come to you and make our home with you' (John 14:23).

CHAPTER TWO

JESUS' CONTEMPORARIES AND THEIR IMAGE OF GOD

In Genesis 1:1 to 2:4, the priests responsible for the introduction to the primeval narrative (Genesis 1-11) were responding to the shock they experienced during their exile in Babylon at the primitive nature of the religion they witnessed there.

> Their idols are silver and gold,
>   the work of human hands.
> They have mouths, but do not speak;
>   eyes, but do not see.
> They have ears, but do not hear;
>   noses, but do not smell.
> They have hands, but do not feel;
>   feet, but do not walk;
>   they make no sound in their throats.
> Those who make them are like them;
>   so are all who trust in them. (Psalm 115:4-8)

For the Israelites, God was responsible for creating the universe and for sustaining everything in being. Everything exists because God wills it to be, and, because God is good, they believed that everything is fundamentally good, indeed 'very good' (Genesis 1:31). This was especially true for human beings who are created 'in the image and likeness of God' (Genesis 1:26). This raises two questions. First, what was their image of God, and secondly, in what ways are we human beings actually in God's image?

Monotheism

The God of Israel is the God who, through Moses, led the Hebrews out of slavery in Egypt, formed them into a nation with its own Law (the Torah), and led them to the Promised Land. Initially, it was their belief that the God of their nation was the greatest of the gods. This gave way to the conviction that their God was the only God, with the implication that other so-called gods are not gods at all.

The implications of monotheism are immense. The monotheist recognises that it is the one God who reveals God's presence in every place, every event, and every person. Hence the many and at first glance rather confusing images of God that we find in the Hebrew scriptures. The way God treated the first-born of the Israelites would lead one to think of God as a God of love. But what does one make of God's treatment of the Egyptians? What is God really like? God is like a mother who cares for the baby in her womb (Isaiah 49:15), yet God is thought of as blessing the person who dashes the baby of the enemy against a rock (Psalm 137:9). What is God really like? If God is at the heart of everything while remaining mysteriously beyond everything, it is difficult not to end up with an understanding of God as being infinitely and powerfully every trait that we can imagine. The net result can be utter confusion, and people can find texts from the Bible to support almost any position that they wish to or feel obliged to adopt. From a superficial glance, the God of Israel seems to be both forgiving and unforgiving, both caring and cruel, both generous and jealous.

This seems to be reflected in the very name 'Israel', which popular etymology translated as 'he who struggles with God'. Because the Israelites believed that there is only one God, who is ultimately responsible for whatever happens in this world, they were locked in an eternal struggle of mind and heart with this God, a struggle which did not allow them to opt for a simple definition of what they recognised as being beyond the limits of their comprehension. At the same time the many images of God that we discover in the Bible are not all equally important, nor are they random. The Israelite had a definite perspective and point of view.

God is Liberator

The central and normative image of God is found in the text that describes the revelation to Moses: the scene of the burning bush (Exodus 3). Moses had been reared in the Egyptian court away from the degradation and slavery experienced by his compatriots. The first chapters of the Book of Exodus record how he came in touch with their condition, how it angered him, how he killed an Egyptian slave driver, and how he subsequently had to flee for his life. For the first time he knew what it was like to be a fugitive. More than that, he knew that he was the only one who had the capacity to help his people. He had contacts in high places in Egypt, a fact that reinforced the call to go back and try to do something about the condition of the Hebrews. He ran from this call, until finally, one day in the desert, he could run no longer. He was caught up in an encounter with God. Frequently, the Bible describes such encounters in the symbolic language of the glory-cloud (*shekinah*) that surrounds people, taking them into the mysterious presence, but without enabling them to 'see' God. In Moses' case, the encounter occurred in the desert, and the glory-cloud appeared in a 'burning bush' (Exodus 3:2).

The opening words of God to Moses give us the central image of the God of Israel. Every other image must be consistent with this and must be understood in relation to it: 'I have seen the miserable state of my people in Egypt. I have heard their appeal to be free of their slave drivers. Yes, I am well aware of their sufferings. I mean to deliver them!' (Exodus 3:7). Before all else, God is redeemer. God led the Israelites out of slavery on a journey of liberation. God took them from a life of slavery to a 'Promised Land'. They were slaves; now they are free, and all because of the power of their God, their redeemer. Whatever else God is, God is the one who cannot stand oppression. Presented with this revelation of God, and the summons to liberate his people, Moses held back, but God replied: 'I will be with you' (*'ehyeh 'immak*, Exodus 3:12). Moses then asked for God's name. He wants to know in what way this God relates to him and his people. The answer gives us our most profound insight into the spirituality of Israel. It comes in two stages.

The first is a promise: *'ehyeh asher 'ehyeh*. 'This is what you must say to the children of Israel: *'ehyeh* has sent me to you ... YHWH has sent me to you' (Exodus 3:14-15). Obviously, the author is here linking the word YHWH with *'ehyeh*. The Greek (Septuagint) translation has *ego eimi ho on* ('I am the being'). The *Jerusalem Bible* English translation has 'I am who I am'. We could retain the future meaning of *'ehyeh* found in Exodus 3:12 and translate 'I will be who I will be'. What we have here is not a name but a promise. God is asking for faith, telling Moses to walk and God will be with him, God will be for him. Moses will come to know God by walking with God. He will come to know who God is as he engages in the task of the Exodus. God promises Moses that he will be with him, and that he will liberate the people from slavery. Moses wants security before he starts. God makes a covenant, a promise, and asks Moses to trust him.

To establish a basis for such a trust, God makes a second statement. It is a call to Moses and to the people to remember: 'You are to say to the children of Israel: YHWH, the God of your ancestors, the God of Abraham, the God of Isaac, and the God of Jacob, has sent me to you' (Exodus 3:15). The fidelity of God can be seen if we look to our past. God was present, calling, supporting, loving. The God of our future, in whom we are asked to trust, is the God of our past whose fidelity has been established. The God of Israel, then, is primarily a Redeemer, who ransoms slaves and liberates them. The word fits perfectly the historical experience that was the beginning of the national identity of Israel.

God redeems people not only from slavery. God liberates us from anything that impedes fullness of life, in other words from 'sin'. Before proceeding let us try to establish what we mean when we speak of 'sin'.

The slavery of sin

Coming from God's hand, creation, which reaches perfection with human beings, is 'very good' (Genesis 1:31). As the primeval narrative states, human beings live because, though formed from dust, God breathes into them God's own spirit (Genesis 2:7). We are created to live our life in a garden (Genesis

2:8), a paradise with fruit trees and fountains, where we can enjoy close communion with God (Genesis 3:8).

Yet it is not at all obvious that people are, in fact, 'very good', and we don't live in a paradise (Genesis 3:24). Brother kills brother (Genesis 4). 'The LORD saw that the wickedness of humankind was great in the earth, and that every inclination of the thoughts of their hearts was only evil continually. And the LORD was sorry that he had made humankind on the earth, and it grieved him to his heart. So the LORD said, "I will blot out from the earth the human beings I have created – people together with animals and creeping things and birds of the air, for I am sorry that I have made them" (Genesis 6:5-7). A return to chaos was held back because of the goodness of one man, Noah (Genesis 6:8). Even so 'the human heart is evil from youth' (Genesis 8:21).

We are created to live in a paradise of intimate communion with God. According to the primeval narrative, this is not our experience because we want to decide for ourselves what is good for us, instead of listening to and waiting on God (Genesis 3:1-7). We think we can build our own way to heaven (Genesis 11:1-9). Cutting ourselves off from God, we lose the harmony we should have with God, and so with nature, with others and with ourselves.

To grasp the meaning of 'sin', let us imagine a world in which everyone's deepest needs are being answered by a resounding 'yes'; a world, in other words, where there is no 'slavery', in which everyone is surrounded by love, a faithful love that gives unconditional care and nurturing to all. In such a world we would all learn to 'be-lieve', that is, we would all choose to 'be-in-love'. We would learn to trust, and our trust would not be betrayed. We would mature and grow in this love, and in our turn we would be able to provide a space where others could experience being loved, and where they could learn to give love. Our whole world would be a garden and a home for people. If you can imagine that, you can imagine a world without sin, a 'Garden of Eden', a paradise.

'Sin' is a very general word for anything and everything that introduces a negative note into this picture we have painted. The word used in the Greek Bible is *hamartia*, which literally translated means 'missing the mark'. It is used of a person who is in the bush and has lost their way. This basic meaning is extended to include anyone who is in any way lost or alienated. The fact is that as soon as we are born we are surrounded not just with love and fidelity but also with non-love and infidelity. The fact is that we learn not only to trust, but to distrust. The fact is that we are not only told the truth and led by those who love us along the path of a maturing ability to love; we are also deceived and distracted, and we develop habits that make us withdraw from love. The fact is that we grow, not only to be able to give love to others, but also to be able to withhold love from others. It is not my intention here to blame everything on what we inherit or on our environment, though these do have a major role to play in our development. Rather it is my intention to hint at the many ways in which sin affects our lives. There is a lot that prevents us from being in love, and the journey to freedom from these barriers and distractions can be long and arduous. We can blame our environment, as we have seen, for a lot of the trouble, but there is also our inherited genetic make-up, and, perhaps, most influential of all, our own incomprehensible ability to say 'no' to the love we need, even when we know we need it, and are able to say 'yes'.

The word 'sin' is used here for all that distracts us from truth and from love. When we are not responsible for this, we call it 'original sin', for it is part of our origins, part of the human condition into which we are born. When we are responsible, we call it 'personal sin'. But whether it is our fault or not – and it is often very difficult to know in any particular instance where the 'blame' lies – we are lost in sin and need to find our way back to the track. The God of Israel, who redeemed Israel from the slavery of Egypt, is before all else the God who redeems people from 'sin', from any enslavement that inhibits fullness of life.

YHWH, *the Saviour*

Another word for this is the word 'saviour'. A saviour is one who makes us 'safe', either by preserving us from whatever might harm us, or, if we have already been harmed, by rescuing us from harm and healing us of its effects. The God of Israel, the one and only God, is the saviour of humankind: 'that people may know and believe me and understand that it is I. No God was formed before me. No God will be after me. I, I am YHWH. There is no other saviour but me' (Isaiah 43:10-11).

It was in YHWH, the faithful one, the redeemer, that the people of Israel ultimately placed their hope. God was their salvation. In God they experienced security; in God they were safe. God pitched God's tent among them, and they were at home with God. It was intimacy with God that mattered most to them. When they thought of life, they thought of union with God. God was the source of their freedom and gave meaning to their existence. These concepts are summed up in the word 'salvation'. God the redeemer is also 'saviour'.

YHWH, *the God of ḥesed we 'emet*

There are two words that keep recurring in the sacred writings as expressing the essential characteristics of God. They are the Hebrew words ḥesed and 'emet. God is often called 'ḥesed we 'emet' (see, for example, Psalms 25:10; 40:12; 57:3, 10; 61:7; 85:10; 86:15; 89:14; 115:1; 138:2). 'ḥesed' is that quality in a community that gives it firm cohesion. One may translate it as 'covenant love'. The commitment given in marriage is an example of 'ḥesed'. In the New Testament, we find the term 'grace' used in the same sense. The 'grace of God' is the love that God has for us which is our security and which binds us together as a people committed to witness to this love. 'emet is a quality that enables others to put their trust in a person. One may translate it 'fidelity'. The Book of Exodus tells us of Moses' prayer to see the glory of God. God promises to reveal God's glory to him and when Moses ascends the mountain, we are told that: 'YHWH passed before him and proclaimed, 'YHWH, YHWH, a God of tenderness and compassion, slow to anger, rich in kindness and faithfulness (ḥesed we 'emet)' (Exodus 34:6).

Moses reminds the people of this steadfast love of YHWH as he gives them his last will and testament. He calls on the people to continue the mission from God to redeem and liberate. It is a call to act justly: 'It is God who sees justice done for the orphan and the widow, who loves the stranger and gives them food and clothing. Love the stranger then, for you were strangers in the land of Egypt' (Deuteronomy 10:18). Again and again the psalms refer to God in these terms. God stands in the divine assembly as the One who dispenses justice: 'No more mockery of justice, no more favouring the wicked! Let the weak and the orphan have justice, be fair to the wretched and destitute; rescue the weak and needy, save them from the clutches of the wicked!' (Psalm 82:1-4).

The message of the prophets is the same. A powerful witness to this is given by the temple singers who are responsible for chapters 40 to 56 of the Isaiah scroll. On their return from exile, they were faced with a community that was in danger of forgetting the universal call, and of narrowing their religion down to national interests such as self-defence, law, ritual and cult. Chapter 56 opens with a magnificent call to justice and to compassionate care for the oppressed among them, including foreigners. The whole of the opening passage merits close attention. It concludes with the words: 'It is the LORD YHWH who speaks, who gathers the outcasts of Israel: there are others I will gather besides those already gathered' (Isaiah 56:8).

There are other images that we should consider. They thought of God as almighty according to their understanding of power. They thought of God, therefore, as controlling everything. They thought of the darkness and chaos in the world as God's punishment for people's failure to obey God's commands. They thought of God as taking their side in conflicts, because their enemies were assumed to be God's enemies. If God did not side with them, they concluded that God was punishing them for failing to abide by the covenant with God to which they had committed themselves.

Let us conclude our brief study of the God of Israel by meditating on a passage from the Isaiah scroll. Faced with a sincere religious people who were following the observances of the Law but who were not experiencing the intimate presence of God in their lives, the writers proclaimed this message from God:

> They seek me day after day. They long to know my
> ways, like a nation that wants to act with integrity and

not ignore the law of its God. They ask me for laws that are just, they long for God to draw near: Why should we fast if you never see it, why do penance if you never notice? (Isaiah 58:2-3).

Drawing on ancient tradition, the basic religious experience of Israel expressed so powerfully in the Exodus account of the burning bush, they challenged the people:

> Fasting like yours today will never make your voice heard on high. Is that the sort of fast that pleases me, hanging your head like a reed, lying down on sackcloth and ashes? Is that what you call fasting, a day acceptable to Yahweh? Is not this the sort of fast that pleases me – it is the LORD YHWH who speaks – to break unjust fetters and undo the thongs of the yoke, to let the oppressed go free, and break every yoke, to share your bread with the hungry, and shelter the homeless poor, to clothe the person you see to be naked and not turn from your own kin? Then will your light shine like the dawn and your wound be quickly healed. Your integrity will go before you and the glory of YHWH behind you. Cry, and YHWH will answer; call, and he will say "I am here". If you do away with the yoke, the clenched fist, the wicked word, if you give your bread to the hungry, and relief to the oppressed, your light will rise in the darkness, and your shadows become like noon, Yahweh will always guide you, giving you relief in desert places. He will give strength to your bones and you will be like a watered garden, like a spring of water whose waters never run dry. (Isaiah 58:4-11)

This is the God who calls the people of Israel in the depths of their life-experience. It is the breath ('Spirit') of this God that breathes life into their world (Genesis 2:7), and that constantly re-creates it (Psalm 104:30). The prophets, who were open to God's call, heard God's word and saw revealed God's presence and will. The key revelation, the central religious insight, was that God is a redeemer. It is their God, the only God, who redeemed them from Egypt, who formed them into a people, who led them through the desert and brought them to the Promised Land. Not all the sacred writings are faithful to this insight. At times the image of God is obscured. But the vital thrust is there all the time, providing perspective and calling the people of Israel to forgo their imperfect notions and distracting religious practices and continue their journey up the mountain of God. It was this concept of God that Jesus inherited.

The political situation at the time of Jesus

From 37BC to 4BC, Herod the Great ruled Palestine, from north of the lake of Gennesaret to south of the Dead Sea, and from the Mediterranean in the west to the east bank of the Jordan river. Shortly after the birth of Jesus, Herod died and his kingdom was divided among his sons. Galilee in the north was ruled by Herod Antipas. The principal town in Galilee was Sepphoris, just a few kilometres from Nazareth where a certain carpenter, Joseph, his wife Mary, and their son Jesus, were living. The largest portion of Herod's kingdom, which included Judaea, Samaria and Idumea, was ruled by Herod Antipas' older brother, Archelaus.

In 6AD, when Jesus was a young boy, Archelaus was removed from power by the Roman Senate, and the Roman army marched into Palestine under the command of a military prefect, Coponius. He introduced taxation, appointed a new High Priest, and brought the people under direct Roman rule. Resistance was immediate and violent. A Galilean called Judas led the revolt. It was crushed mercilessly. The Romans won the war, but the national liberation movement was born, and all through Jesus' life, resistance to the occupying army festered just below the surface. It erupted into full-scale war only a generation after Jesus' death, and culminated in the destruction of Jerusalem in 70AD.

This was the violent world in which Jesus lived and taught. People's minds went back to the years recorded in the Book of Jeremiah when the Babylonians burnt their city to the ground, destroyed and desecrated the temple, and took their ancestors into captivity in Babylon. With Jeremiah, they interpreted that catastrophe as a punishment of God for their sins: 'I, YHWH, will bring disaster on this place, because the people have abandoned me, have profaned this place, filled this place with the blood of the innocent, burnt their sons and daughters there. The valley of Ben Hinnom (*'Gehenna'*) will be a valley of slaughter, the city will be a desolation, a derision, a burial ground for lack of other space since they have grown so stubborn and refused to listen to my words' (Jeremiah 19). It seemed that those years were upon them again.

Yet people's minds also went back to more recent events: the successful war waged by the Maccabees against the Syrian king. On that occasion, the city and temple were saved by the courageous fidelity of those who pledged themselves to total purity of religion. Could this happen again? Everywhere there was a heightened expectation that God would soon intervene in their world, and deliver them from the Romans, destroying all evil, and finally bringing about God's reign. This expectation took many forms, but there was a general mood of waiting for the coming of the last days, for the eschatological prophet, for the final judgment of God.

The prevailing expectation was that God's judgment would be a destructive one. In anger, God would destroy all evil: the Romans, of course; but could it also involve, as it had once before, the temple? Would there be another *gehenna*? What would be left when God's destroying angel had completed his task? If they were repentant, if they followed the Law, if they fought for the purity of their religion, would God spare them? Could they be a remnant, saved from the judgment? After all, they were God's chosen people, and the faithful God would honour God's promises!

It was into such a world that Jesus came and preached an ancient, but new, message: God is a redeemer, not a destroyer. God wills to save, not condemn. It is not a matter of avoiding God's judgment, but of welcoming it. We are not to hope to be saved *from* it, but saved *by* it. Jesus spoke about gehenna ('hell'), for he saw the way in which his contemporaries were heading. He warned them of what would happen to them if they did not recognise God's gift of peace (Luke 19:42). However, his preaching was 'good news' because he taught them that all God's power was among them to save, not to destroy. Destruction, if it happened, would be self-destruction that followed on a stubborn refusal of God's salvation. This message stands out in clearer relief against the background of the message being preached by other religious groups at the time.

Jesus and the Zealots

The Zealots were working for the violent overthrow of Roman occupation. They were confident that the Jews were the chosen race. God's imminent judgment would be realised, according to their way of thinking, through their courage, determination and self-sacrifice. They were willing to fight to the end to defend the honour of their nation, and so the honour of their God. How different Jesus' teaching was from theirs. The critical difference was that Jesus spoke of God as the Father of *all*. Listen to his words about how we should relate to our enemies: 'You have learned how it was said: You must love your neighbour (see Leviticus 19:18) and hate your enemy. But I say this to you: love your enemies and pray for those who persecute you; in this way you will be children of your Father in heaven, for he causes his sun to rise on bad people as well as good, and his rain to fall on honest and dishonest people alike. You must be perfect just as your heavenly Father is perfect' (Matthew 5:43, 48). Jesus worked and prayed for a peace that would come through people recognising that every person is precious in the eyes of the one Father, that every race is a chosen race. Peacemakers were especially blessed 'for they shall be called children of God' (Matthew 5:9). Peace ('*shalom*') was possible as a result of God's imminent reign, but it could come only if the people changed their outlook ('repented'). Jesus revealed the universal Fatherhood of God, and the consequent commandment of unconditional, universal forgiveness and love. He accepted no compromise.

It was when he realised that the Zealots, and others who shared their view, were determined to pursue their violent course that Jesus had to face the fact that in this, at least, his mission had failed. Luke records his lament over the city: 'As Jesus drew near and came in sight of the city he shed tears over it and said: "If you in your turn had only understood on this day the message of peace! But, alas, it is hidden from your eyes! Yes, a time is coming when your enemies will raise fortifications all round you, when they will encircle you and hem you in on every side. They will dash you and the children inside your walls to the ground; they will leave not one stone standing on another within you – and all because you did not recognise your opportunity when God offered it'" (Luke 19:41-44). But Jesus himself continued to preach and to offer peace, and he kept forgiving his enemies right to the end (Luke 23:34). He also left his followers the instruction to 'make disciples of all the nations' (Matthew 28:19), telling them all of the universal Father, whose love is revealed most powerfully in his relationship with Jesus, his Son, and whose Holy Spirit is at work in the world reconciling all people to each other and to God.

Jesus and the Sadducees

The main opposition to Jesus seems to have come from the Sadducees, made up of the priestly aristocracy and the leading families. They saw themselves as bearing the responsibility for preserving intact the ancient and orthodox traditions of Israel. Their main concern, as one would expect, was for the exact observance of temple cult. They were pragmatists, and, unlike the Zealots, favoured accommodation with Rome. This was partly because it was they who received most benefit from the Roman occupation.

Temple worship had its place in Judaism. The prophets, however, were constantly reminding the people that the worship they offered was worship offered to God, and so could not be a substitute for doing God's will in working for the redemption of the poor and needy (Amos 5:21-25, Jeremiah 7:1-11; Isaiah 56:1-8). Jesus followed in this tradition. He cleared the temple in a powerful prophetic gesture of displeasure (John 2:13-22; Mark 11:12-33; Matthew 21:12-27; Luke 19:45 – 20:8). His reasons for doing so are given in the Synoptic Gospels by referring back to the criticism of temple worship given by Jeremiah and Isaiah. According to Jesus, the temple was meant to be a 'house of prayer' (Mark 11:17 = Isaiah 56:7) and 'for all the nations' (Jeremiah 7:11). The Sadducees failed to recognise the universal Fatherhood of God; they also failed to be instruments of God's redemptive justice reaching to the ends of the earth and to outcasts. For Jesus, worship was something that was possible for all (John 4:21-24). It was also to be an expression and celebration of religious dedication to God and to God's reign, and not an institutionalised routine that went on without regard either to genuine prayer or to justice.

Jesus and the Pharisees

Jesus had far more interaction with another religious group, the Pharisees. They were concerned with fidelity to God's will as expressed in the written and oral Law. They were zealous nationalists, having originated in the movement that overthrew Syrian rule in the first part of the second century BC. They were determined to uphold Jewish language, Jewish customs, and above all total reverence for God and for God's will. They insisted on the need for a total purification of life in accordance with the Law. As a sect within Judaism, their influence went beyond their numbers. Many of them were scribes, learned in the Law, and because as laymen they were close to the ordinary people, they exercised considerable influence through their preaching and example.

Jesus shared with them a consuming passion to do the will of God (Mark 3:35 and 14:36). However, he soon came into open conflict with them over their interpretation of that will.

Besides accusing many of them of hypocrisy (Mark 7:1-13 and Matthew 23), he confronted them, because, as he saw matters, they had missed the central meaning of the Law (Matthew 9:13 and 12:7): they had failed to appreciate God's love. Their insisting on the observance of the Law was placing a burden on people, increasing people's fears and reinforcing an image of God that was at variance with what Jesus knew as the genuine tradition of Israel.

The Pharisees believed that the only hope for the people was to bear patiently and faithfully the yoke of the Law. Here it is enough to note the clear contrast between Jesus and the Pharisees in this regard. Matthew records Jesus as saying: 'Come to me, all you who labour and are overburdened, and I will give you rest. Shoulder my yoke and learn from me, for I am gentle and humble in heart, and you will find rest for your souls. Yes, my yoke is easy and my burden light' (Matthew 11:28-30). This is the 'good news'. Luke gives us an impression of the contrast when he writes: 'The tax collectors and the sinners were all seeking Jesus' company to hear what he had to say, and the Pharisees and the Scribes complained: 'This man', they said, 'welcomes sinners and eats with them' (Luke 15:1-2). The Sabbath was a day of special consecration to God. Jesus by-passed petty regulations whenever compassion called for it. The Beloved Disciple tells of one occasion when Jesus healed a man in Jerusalem, and he adds the comment: 'It was because he did things like this on the Sabbath that the Jews began to persecute Jesus' (John 5:16). We get the same impression from the other Gospels (Mark 3:1-6). The 'good news' was that 'the Sabbath was made for human beings, not human beings for the Sabbath' (Mark 2:27). God is for us, and all the regulations of the Law must witness to the redeeming and saving will of God.

Jesus and the Essenes

Another group who shared many of the convictions of the Pharisees were the Essenes. They considered the world to be so wicked and unredeemable that they fled from it and set up their own communities in the desert. There they set up a lifestyle that they considered to be totally faithful to God. Jesus, on the contrary, saw the imminent reign of God as holding out the possibility of redemption especially to the outcasts and the sinners, and he moved among them as a doctor might move among the sick (Mark 2:17), encouraging, healing, liberating and challenging them to allow the love of God to break into their lives (see Luke 5:30, 15:1-2). The Beloved Disciple expresses this truth in the following words: 'God loved the world so much that he gave his only Son, so that everyone who believes in him may not be lost but may have eternal life. For God sent his Son into the world not to condemn the world, but so that through him the world might be saved' (John 3:16-17).

The Good News brought by Jesus was that God was not about to destroy the world, whether by flood or by fire. God is the Redeemer and Saviour. God is the life-giver, not the life-destroyer. We can destroy ourselves by refusing to believe the good news, and by obstinately ignoring or turning our back on God's saving love. But the love is present, powerfully active in healing and liberating. And it is for the whole world. Far from fleeing the world, Jesus loved it into faith, or tried to. His being murdered is a measure of his failure. The way he died is a measure of his success. For he, at any rate, believed in a God who loved to the end, and he gave his life in that belief.

Jesus and John the Baptist

Finally, let us examine the preaching of the prophet John. John sensed that his world was on the verge of collapse, and that he was preaching at the end of an age. He sensed that history was repeating itself, only this time God's judgment would be final. In line with current expectations, John envisaged God's judgment as a destructive one. John summoned the whole of Israel to repent and by fidelity to justice to be a remnant that would be spared God's avenging judgment: 'His winnowing-fan is in his hand; he will clear his threshing-floor and gather his wheat into the barn; but the chaff he will burn in a fire that will never go out' (Matthew 3:12). 'Even now the axe is laid to the roots of the trees, so that any tree which fails to produce good fruit will be cut down and thrown on the fire' (Matthew 3:10).

In many ways, Jesus was very close to John. The first decision of Jesus recorded in the Gospels was when 'he came from Galilee to the Jordan and was baptised by John' (Matthew 3:13). A number of Jesus' early disciples came to him from John (John 1:35), and before John's imprisonment Jesus seems to have followed John's practice of inviting people to be baptised (John 3:22-26). Matthew even uses an identical expression to summarise the preaching of John and the preaching of Jesus: 'Repent, for the kingdom of heaven is close at hand' (Matthew 3:2 and 4:17). Jesus recognised John as a prophet (Matthew 11:9) and clearly admired him: 'I tell you solemnly, of all the children born of women, a greater than John the Baptist has never been seen' (Matthew 11:11).

However, as we will see in the following chapter, Jesus and his good news was different even from John's.

CHAPTER THREE

JESUS' IMAGE OF GOD

Jesus' disciples found in him the answer to the need and the longing that fills the pages of the Old Testament. Here at last was a human being who was truly 'in God's image and likeness'. Walter Kasper writes: 'Whenever something new arises, whenever life is awakened and reality reaches ecstatically beyond itself, in all seeking and striving, in every ferment and birth, and even more in the beauty of creation, something of the being and activity of God's Spirit is manifested' (*The God of Jesus Christ*, page 227). This divine activity came to perfect flowering in Jesus of Nazareth. Denis Edwards writes: 'God gives to creatures themselves the capacity for the new. Because of God's creative and redeeming presence to creatures, they can become something they were not. When matter comes to life on earth, when life becomes self-conscious and personal, this occurs through God enabling creation to transcend itself and become something new. Above all when one of us in the human and creaturely community, Jesus of Nazareth, is so radically open to God, so one with God, that we rightly see him as God-with-us, then we can say that in this person creation transcends itself into God' (*How God Acts*, page 158).

There is something very different about Jesus, and it is to this difference that we will now turn, for it takes us to the heart of Jesus' thinking about God, and gives us an insight into Jesus' own personality. Jesus shared the faith of his people.

He was faithful to the religious insights we described in the previous chapter. He penetrated to their deepest meaning. He also revealed God in a manner that, while faithful to the religion of Israel, went beyond it. Jesus' teaching about God came as a surprise to his contemporaries, as something quite unexpected. Jesus showed how wrong in some ways was the image of God held and taught by the religious leaders of his day.

The first indication that Jesus had a message that was different even from that of the Baptist comes early in Mark's Gospel: 'One day when John's disciples and the Pharisees were fasting, some people came and said to Jesus: Why is it that John's disciples and the disciples of the Pharisees fast, but your disciples do not?' (Mark 2:18). Jesus' reply is most instructive: 'Surely, the bridegroom's attendants would never think of fasting while the bridegroom is still with them?' (Mark 2:19). Like John, Jesus could see signs of an approaching catastrophe for his nation. Unless people made a radical conversion towards God, he could foresee the approaching end to his world (he seems to have shown no interest in the speculative point about the end of *the* world: see Mark 13:32, Acts 1:7). Like John, he looked to God to bring about redemption once again for his people. He sensed that he was living at a crucial time (Mark 1:15), a time when God's judgment would soon be manifest. But he was not expecting God to come from outside, as it were, to destroy the wicked world, as did John and the others who shared his expectations. If Jerusalem was to be destroyed, if the people were to go through another hell (*'gehenna'*) this would not be an act of God's punishing justice. Rather, it would be the result of people's refusal to listen to Jesus' message of peace (Luke 13:34-35 and 19:41-44).

For Jesus, the judgment of God is the judgment of the 'bridegroom'. The 'reign of God' that he sensed to be 'close at hand' (Mark 1:15) was the release of the active power of God, the Redeemer and Saviour, the Lover of humankind. This is what made Jesus' message 'good news' (Mark 1:15). Insofar as the world was wicked, God's powerful presence (the 'Spirit') was there, not to condemn and destroy, like an axe, or a fire, but to forgive, purify and save (John 3:17). Insofar as the world was confused, God was present to enlighten. Insofar as the world was paralysed, deaf and blind, God was present to heal. Matthew and Luke both record the following incident: 'Now John in his prison had heard what Christ was doing and he sent his disciples to ask him: Are you the one who is to come, or must we wait for someone else?' Jesus answered, 'Go back and tell John what you hear and see; the blind see again, the lame walk, lepers are cleansed, the deaf hear, the dead are raised to life and the Good News is proclaimed to the poor;· and happy is the person who does not lose faith in me' (Matthew 11:2-6: see Luke 7:18-23).

At the beginning of his Gospel, Mark gets to the heart of Jesus' teaching: 'Jesus came to Galilee, proclaiming the good news of God, and saying: The time is fulfilled. The reign of God has come near. Repent. Believe the good news' (Mark 1:14-15). Jesus is calling people to repent, that is, to think differently, especially about God. The good news is that God is Love and that God is calling everyone to enjoy communion with God. It is welcoming this that makes repentance possible. Mark writes: 'They went to Capernaum; and when the Sabbath came, Jesus entered the synagogue and taught. They were astounded at his teaching, for he taught them as one having authority, and not like the scribes' (Mark 1:21-22). Jesus' teaching about God flowed from his experience, from his heart. Mark records the scene when the disciples return from their first mission. Jesus invites them to come aside with him for a while, so they get into boats and row to a deserted place. But people hear about it and reach the spot before them. Mark writes: 'As Jesus went ashore, he saw a great crowd; and he had compassion for them, because they were like sheep without a shepherd; and he began to teach them at some length' (Mark 6:34). Jesus' teaching was so powerful because people felt that it flowed from his compassion,

Luke writes: 'Filled with the power of the Spirit, Jesus returned to Galilee, and a report about him spread through all the surrounding countryside. He began to teach in their synagogues and was praised by everyone' (Luke 4:14-15). Luke then portrays Jesus reading from Isaiah in the synagogue of Nazareth. Jesus found the place in the scroll where it is written: "The Spirit of the LORD is upon me because he has anointed me to bring good news to the poor. He has sent me to proclaim release from captives and recovery of sight to the blind, to let the oppressed go free" ' (Luke 4:16-21). The good news is that God wants us to be freed from everything that distracts us and holds us bound. God wants us to 'live and live to the full' (John 10:10).

Jesus taught in words what he demonstrated in his life. In examining his teaching about God, we are, at the same time, exploring his relationship to his Father. His key teaching is that God is 'Father', and that it is possible for us, woman or man, to be 'sons' of God in the sense that Jesus shares with us his experience of being son: his communion with his Father. We are graced to share Jesus' own communion with God, his Spirit.

While others were placing their hope in fidelity to the Law and in exact observance and ritual purity, in the hope that those who behaved thus would be spared when God in his justice destroyed the world by fire, Jesus was working to bring about the conversion of his world by revealing God's love, and he was inspiring others to join him in deeds of love born of prayer.

Another saying of Jesus recorded by both Luke and Matthew helps us understand how Jesus understood his mission in relation to John the Baptist. 'Up to the time of John it was the Law and the Prophets; since then, the kingdom of God has been preached, and by violence everyone is getting in' (Luke 16:16; see also Matthew 11:12-13). Jesus was aware of the determination of his Father to redeem his people, and of the violence that God's love was doing to the limited expectations of the religious authorities including John. Nothing was going to be able to stand in the way of God's love. There was room for everyone in the community drawn together by Jesus. The power of God's Spirit was working through him, not to destroy, not to uphold the limited regulations of the tradition, but to heal and to save. It was this conviction that showed itself in his actions. It was this conviction that inspired all his teaching about God.

From a number of points of view, Jesus failed. He himself was killed and only a generation after his crucifixion, his land was ravaged by war. His worst fears were realised. Towards the end of his short ministry, his failure bore in upon him and we find him weeping over the city (Luke 19:41) and undergoing his own personal agony (Luke 22:41-44). But the story of Christianity is the story of Jesus' success. Some listened to his teaching and believed him. He had said once: 'I have come to bring fire to the earth, and how I wish it were blazing already' (Luke 12:49). He started a fire in people's hearts, and, in spite of his own short-term failure to avert the 'hell' that was threatening, he left his contemporaries with what the Beloved Disciple calls 'the way, the truth, and the life' (John 14:6): the way of prayer that issues in love. Jesus gives us an example in his prayer 'Father, may your reign come, your will be done on earth as in heaven' (Matthew 6:9-10); the truth that God is our Father; the life of intimacy with God that enables us, as it enabled him, to live Life to the full even amid failure.

Mark states that his purpose in writing is to present 'the good news of Jesus the Messiah, the Son of God' (Mark 1:1). His focus throughout is on Jesus as God's Messiah and Son. When we watch Jesus and listen to him, we are watching God act and speak through him, for God is Jesus' Father: the source of all that Jesus is and says and does. It is Jesus' mission to reveal God by bringing about the 'reign of God'. It is God who liberates through Jesus. It is God who heals through Jesus. It is God whose compassionate love we see as we watch Jesus (Mark 6:34). It is God who invites everyone (Mark 11:17) to enjoy living in God's kingdom, and to contribute to it (Mark 12:41-44) by opening our hearts to receive and give love. Mark's presentation of what God is teaching and doing through Jesus reaches its climax when Jesus gives his life in love from the cross. The curtain that veils our eyes is torn asunder (Mark 15:38) and now anyone who looks can see God revealed as Self-giving Love.

Matthew adds some sayings of Jesus that reveal Jesus' image of God. Jesus invites us to love our enemies, because God loves them (Matthew 5:45-48). God is the one who provides 'our daily bread' (Matthew 6:11). God loves to forgive (Matthew 6:12; 18:27). Jesus draws our attention to the power and beauty of creation as a revelation of God (Matthew 6:26-30; 10:29). God is our 'Father', the source of all we are (Matthew 11:27). God has compassion for the stray sheep (Matthew 18:13-14). Jesus' favourite image for the kind of world God wants everyone to enjoy is a wedding banquet (Matthew 22:9).

Luke assures us that Jesus brings good news to the poor, frees captives and enlightens, because he is anointed by God and sent for that purpose (Luke 4:18, 43). In other words, it is God who is revealed in Jesus' ministry. God does not reject sinners; God calls us to change, to open ourselves to welcome God's love (Luke 5:32). Jesus calls us to 'be compassionate, just as your Father is compassionate' (Luke 6:35-36). Jesus is revealing God's judgment. In declaring that his mission is to seek out and save the lost (Luke 19:10), Jesus is revealing his image of God. Jesus goes to the heart of how he sees God in his story of the father and his two boys (Luke 15). The younger boy shows complete disregard for his father's feelings, sells off his heritage and wastes everything in 'dissolute living'. What is the father's (God's) response? Longing, hoping, delight when he sees the son, compassion, love and joy.

Jesus' image of God is so different from that of the religious leaders.

- * They thought that God hated Israel's enemies. The God in whom Jesus believed wants us to 'love your enemies and pray for those who persecute you' (Matthew 5:44). And why? Because 'your Father in heaven makes his sun rise on the evil and on the good, and sends rain on the righteous and on the unrighteous' (Matthew 5:45). They did not picture God as being 'kind to the ungrateful and the wicked' (Luke 6:35). They did not see the Messiah as 'the saviour of the world' (John 4:42), including the despised Samaritans.

* They expected the promised Messiah to liberate Israel as they pictured God liberating their ancestors from slavery in Egypt. They did not expect a gentle Messiah who would invite us: 'Come to me, all you that are weary and are carrying heavy burdens, and I will give you rest. Take my yoke upon you, and learn from me; for I am gentle and humble in heart, and you will find rest for your souls' (Matthew 11:28-29). Jesus' disciples watched him, listened to him, and came to acknowledge him as the promised Messiah, a Messiah very different from the one they had been taught to expect (Luke 9:20).

* The religious leaders pictured God according to the way they experienced their rulers, punishing anyone who does not obey their will. They did not expect one who would not 'break a bruised reed or quench a smouldering wick' (Matthew 12:20). The God in whom Jesus believed was determined to rescue the sheep that strayed from the flock: 'It is not the will of your Father in heaven that one of these little ones should be lost' (Matthew 18:14).

* When a sinful woman anoints Jesus' feet while he is at table at the house of a Pharisee, the Pharisee and his other guests are scandalised. They see her sins. Jesus sees her sins, too, but he sees her love and declares that she must have been forgiven or she could not love so much (Luke 7:47).

* They were shocked at Jesus picturing God as celebrating the return of the prodigal son. They identified with the older brother who was angry

and refused to join in the celebrations (Luke 15:11-32).

* When they caught a woman committing adultery, they saw themselves as being obedient to God in having her stoned to death (Leviticus 20:10). Jesus was not blind to her sin, but the God Jesus knew did not condemn her or punish her in her sin. She was suffering more than enough from the consequences of her behaviour. He loved her that she would find the strength to change her ways (John 8:1-11).

* They saw riches as being a proof of God's favour. They did not expect the Messiah to declare: 'Woe are you who are rich' (Luke 6:24), and 'you cannot serve God and wealth' (Luke 16:13).

* Because they were afraid of leprosy, they thought that they were obeying God by banishing from the community people who might have the disease (see Leviticus 13:45-46). The God in whom Jesus believed wants to embrace the man, and welcome him back into the community, not banish him (Mark 1:41).

* Because they believed that God controlled whatever was happening, they presumed that people who were paralysed were being punished by God for some sin. Similarly, they thought that a man who was blind from birth must have sinned, or, if not, his parents must have sinned (John 9:2). The God is whom Jesus believed wants to forgive sin, not punish the sinner (Mark 2:5). God wants us to see (John 9:7), and to walk free (Mark 2:11-12).

* They thought God wanted them to keep away from sinners. The God in whom Jesus believed wants people to love us sinners. How else will we see that there is another way to live, and find healing? (Mark 2:15-17).

* They thought God wanted them to obey the laws of fasting, whatever the situation. Jesus respects that there is a place for fasting, but it is much more important that we believe in God's love for us. God wants us to see life as a wedding banquet, a celebration of love (Mark 2:18-22).

* They were convinced that it is God's will to consecrate the Sabbath to God, and they spelt out what was required to do so. Jesus shared their respect, but not when obeying human traditions means that we neglect love and care for others. He was grieved at their hardness of heart (Mark 3:5-6). 'Woe to you, scribes and Pharisees, hypocrites! For you lock people out of the kingdom of heaven. You do not go in yourselves, and when others are going in, you stop them' (Matthew 23:13). 'Woe to you lawyers! For you load people with burdens hard to bear, and you yourselves do not lift a finger to ease them' (Luke 11:46).

* Because of their hardness of heart they refused to listen to Jesus' message. They rejected the peace he was offering. 'How often have I desired to gather your children together as a hen gathers her brood under her wings, and you were not willing' (Matthew 23:37). Jesus could see that this rejection would lead to the destruction of the city and the

temple: 'See, your house is left to you, desolate' (Matthew 23:38). He wept at their failure to welcome the good news that God is love and wants us to welcome that love (Luke 19:41-44).

They saw their role as teaching the people about God and how we are to respond to God. Jesus challenges them: 'Isaiah prophesied rightly about you hypocrites, as it is written: "This people honours me with their lips, but their hearts are far from me; in vain do they worship me, teaching human precepts as doctrine" (Isaiah 29:13). You abandon the commandment of God and hold to human traditions' (Mark 7:6-8). Jesus' teaching was very different because his image of God was very different. 'Jesus saw a great crowd and was moved with compassion for them, because they were like sheep without a shepherd and he set about teaching them at some length' (Mark 6:34). People 'were astounded at Jesus' teaching, for he taught them as one having authority, and not like the scribes' (Mark 1:22).On the whole, the religious leaders persisted in their failure to listen to the good news about God, and they failed to see Jesus as the promised Messiah. They had him crucified, and 'the chief priests, along with the scribes, were also mocking Jesus among themselves and saying, "He saved others; he cannot save himself. Let the Messiah, the King of Israel, come down from the cross now, so that we may see and believe"' (Mark 15:31-32). By rejecting Jesus, they rejected the image of God that he reveals.

CHAPTER FOUR

JESUS' COMMUNION WITH GOD

In this chapter, we focus on Jesus' divinity, on his intimate communion with God, a communion, a divinity, that Jesus wants everyone to share. This communion can be seen in every aspect of Jesus' life. It is particularly obvious when we see him alone in prayer. His prayer is at the heart of what Jesus invites us to share.

Jesus' baptism (Mark 1:9-11; Matthew 3:13-17; Luke 3:21-22; John 1:32-34)

We first meet Jesus when as a young man in his early thirties he joins a crowd who are seeking baptism in the Jordan from the prophet John. They are seeking what everyone is seeking: a communion that refreshes our souls and shows us how to live a life that has more joy than we find when our lives are superficial and distracted. They want to live to the full. So does Jesus. Jesus was 'praying' (Luke 3:21). There was something quite special about Jesus' prayer that day. He had what we would call a mystical experience: a profound experience of being loved by the One he looked to as the source of his being. This experience proved to be a turning point in his life. We know virtually nothing about him prior to this day. After it, we witness a preacher, a healer, and an extraordinary example of love as he gathers disciples around him and begins a movement that we know as the Christian community.

When his disciples looked back on Jesus' experience that day, they spoke in terms of God's Spirit descending on him. To guide us in our reflections on this scene, they point us to a beautiful song-poem in the Isaiah scroll. It begins: 'Here is my servant whom I uphold, my chosen one in whom my soul delights' (Isaiah 42:1 = Mark 1:11). Jesus was so overwhelmed by his experience of being loved that he had to go into the wilderness to discover in silence its significance for him and for others. The poem continues:

> I have put my spirit upon him;
> > he will bring forth justice to the nations.
>
> He will not cry or lift up his voice,
> > or make it heard in the street;
>
> a bruised reed he will not break,
> > and a dimly burning wick he will not quench;
> > he will faithfully bring forth justice.
>
> He will not grow faint or be crushed
> > until he has established justice in the earth;
> > and the coastlands wait for his teaching.
>
> Thus says God, the LORD,
> > who created the heavens and stretched them out,
> > who spread out the earth and what comes from it,
>
> who gives breath to the people upon it
> > and spirit to those who walk in it:
>
> I am the LORD, I have called you in righteousness,
> > I have taken you by the hand and kept you;
> > I have given you as a covenant to the people,

>   a light to the nations,
>   to open the eyes that are blind,
>   to bring out the prisoners from the dungeon,
>   from the prison those who sit in darkness.
>   (Isaiah 42:2-7)

Jesus' disciples found in this song a description of Jesus' life and mission! In the silence of the desert Jesus came to see that everyone needs to experience what he experienced that day at the Jordan. The source of our being, the one who sustains us in existence, says to each of us, 'You are my son/ my daughter whom I uphold, my chosen one in whom my soul delights'. Jesus believed that he was being invited 'to be a light to the nations', to draw everyone to know that God's desire for us is that we know how loved we are. Set free in this way, we would find our unique capacity to welcome and respond to love by sharing Jesus' belief and by loving as Jesus loves: We would indeed be what we are created to be: 'in God's image and likeness.'

Alone with his Abba

After a busy day and night of reaching out in love to the sick, 'at daybreak Jesus departed and went into a deserted place' (Luke 4:42). 'He would withdraw to deserted places and pray' (Luke 5:16). 'Jesus went out to the mountain to pray; and he spent the night in prayer to God' (Luke 6:12). 'Jesus dismissed the crowds and he went up the mountain by himself to pray. When evening came, he was there alone' (Matthew 14:23-24). Jesus' disciples could see that there was something very special about Jesus' prayer: 'He was praying in a certain place, and after he had finished, one of his disciples said to him, "LORD, teach us to pray" (Luke 11:1). They came to realise that it was in prayer that Jesus experienced the communion with God that he was inspired to share with others. It was in prayer that he discovered God's will: 'In the morning, while it was still very dark, Jesus got up and went out to a deserted place, and there he prayed. Simon and his companions hunted for him. When they found him, they said to him, "Everyone is searching for you". He answered, "Let us go on to the neighbouring towns, so that I may proclaim the message there also; for that is what I came out to do". (Mark 1:35-38)

Jesus loved in response to an inspiration that he experienced deep in his consciousness, an inspiration that he believed had its source in God. He was not drawing people to himself. He was drawing them to God. He was drawing them to learn to trust their own hearts and learn to believe, as he believed, how lovable and loved we are.

The Transfiguration (Mark 9:2-8; Matthew 17:1-8; Luke 9:18, 28-36)

Jesus' communion with God radiated out from him. The gospel-writers record an occasion when 'Jesus was praying alone, with only his disciples near him' (Luke 9:18). He turned to them and asked what he meant to them. Peter responded that they believed that Jesus was the Messiah promised to Israel by God. They needed to unlearn much of what they had been taught to expect from the Messiah, so Jesus begins to speak about the suffering that he, and therefore they, would have to face. They could not comprehend what Jesus was telling them.

Six days later, Jesus took with him Peter and James and his brother John and led them up a high mountain, by themselves. And he was transfigured before them, and his face shone like the sun, and his clothes became dazzling white (In the words of Psalm Four 'the light of God's face shone upon him'). Suddenly there appeared to them Moses and Elijah, talking with him. Then Peter said to Jesus: LORD, it is good for us to be here; if you wish, I will make three dwellings here, one for you, one for Moses, and one for Elijah. While he was still speaking, suddenly a bright cloud overshadowed them, and from the cloud a voice said: This is my Son, the Beloved; with him I am well pleased; listen to him! When the disciples heard this, they fell to the ground and were overcome by fear. But Jesus came and touched them, saying: Get up and do not be afraid. And when they looked up, they saw no one except Jesus himself alone. (Matthew 17:1-8)

In this dramatic portrayal of Jesus' prayer on the mountain, the gospel-writers recall Mount Sinai and God's gift of the Torah through Moses and his intimate communion with God 'for forty days and forty nights' (Exodus 24:18). They recall also the prophet Elijah who encountered God in the silence (1 Kings 19:12). Then Moses and Elijah disappear and there is 'only Jesus, God's Beloved Son'. We are to 'listen to him.' In Jesus the Law and the prophets are fulfilled. They have achieved their purpose. They have brought us to Jesus. It is in sharing Jesus' prayer that we share his divinity and enjoy the communion with God that is the goal of our existence.

Jesus prays (Matthew 11:25-27; Luke 10:21-22)

Jesus declared: 'No one knows the Son except the Father, and no one knows the Father except the Son and anyone to whom the Son chooses to reveal him' (Matthew 11:27). Jesus is using the word 'know' in its rich biblical sense. It is not knowing about, nor is it a logical conclusion formed by scrutinising one's experience. Rather it is a knowing that comes from intimate communion. Jesus is speaking of the intimacy of his communion with the God in whom he places his trust, an intimacy that he invites us to know. We are offered a rare insight into the content of Jesus' prayer: 'I thank you, Father, LORD of heaven and earth, because you have revealed these things to infants; yes, Father, for such was your gracious will' (Luke 10:21). Jesus looked on God as his Father (Abba). He identified as a child (a son), and asked us to see ourselves as, like him, totally dependent on our Father.

Teach us how to pray (Luke 11:1)

Jesus' disciples came to realise that the secret of Jesus' life and ministry was to be found in his prayer. Not surprisingly they wanted him to teach them how to pray.

Note

In Chapter Ten, we will explore Jesus' communion with God at the Last Supper and during his agony and dying.

CHAPTER FIVE

JESUS' LOVE

Since everything Jesus is, everything he says, and everything he does, flows from his union with God, and since Jesus knows God as Love (I am using the word 'know' in its biblical meaning of knowing through intimate communion), it is Jesus' love that most characterises him. He wants us to welcome his love, which gives us the space to find ourselves as loved and to trust the mystical experiences that love engenders in us. In giving us his Spirit, Jesus is giving us his love. It is this gift that we share with others. He does not invite us to love like him. He invites us to find our own unique way of experiencing and sharing God's love, and that we might do this he invites us to share his divinity, his communion with God.

The Beloved Disciple speaks of Jesus as being 'in the bosom of the Father' (John 1:18). Peter states: 'We have come to believe and know that you are the Holy One of God' (John 6:69). Jesus says: 'The Father knows me, and I know the Father … The Father loves me' (John 10:15, 17). 'I know him' (John 7:29). 'The Father loves the Son' (John 3:35; 5:20). 'I am in the Father and the Father is in me' (John 14:10). 'The Father is with me' (John 16:32). 'The Father and I are one' (John 10:30). 'I live because of the Father' (John 6:57). 'The Father is in me and I am in the Father' (John 10:38).

It is Jesus' intimate communion with God that flows out in love to people. John the Baptist speaks of Jesus as the 'bridegroom' (John 3:29). Jesus is the one who 'gives the Spirit without measure' (John 3:38). 'I am in my Father, and you in me, and I in you' (John 14:20). 'As the Father has loved me, so I have loved you; abide in my love' (John 15:9).

Let us journey through Jesus' ministry, focusing on his love. In loving people the way he did, Jesus gave meaning to their lives, and at the deepest level of their religious experience. For his love is a revelation of God and an invitation to communion with God.

* Jesus attracts disciples to live and journey with him (Mark 1:16-20; Matthew 4:18-22; Luke 5:1-11; John 1:37-46). Mark and Matthew mention that two pairs of brothers, Simon and Andrew, James and John, accepted Jesus' invitation to leave their fishing trade and accompany him. Luke reflects on Jesus' invitation to Simon. Later, Thomas joins them (Mark 2:14; Matthew 9:9; Luke 5:27-28). In the Gospel of the Beloved Disciple, we hear that Andrew and a companion (is this companion the Beloved Disciple?) spend the afternoon with Jesus and are so impressed that Andrew goes to his brother Simon, and tells him he has just met the Messiah, the one whom God promised to send to fulfil the hopes and longings of Israel. The next day, Jesus goes to Galilee and invites Philip to follow him. Philip then invites Nathanael. We are left to ponder what it was about Jesus that attracted them.

* Jesus' heart goes out to a poor, psychically disturbed man in the synagogue (Mark 1:23-26; Luke 4:33-35). It was Jesus' teaching about God (which came to be called the 'good news') that penetrated the darkness

of the man's psyche. It was Jesus' love that invited the man to believe that God was loving him into life.

* Simon's mother-in-law is able to offer hospitality to Jesus (Mark 1:29-31; Matthew 8:14-15; Luke 4:38-39). She would have heard Simon speak of Jesus. We can imagine how much she was looking forward to meeting him and offering him hospitality, and the disappointment of succumbing to a fever. 'Jesus came, took her by the hand and lifted her up.' How gentle must have been that touch and the healing love that gave her the strength to look after Simon and his companions, and their new friend Jesus.

* Jesus' healing love (Mark 1:34; Matthew 8:16-17; Luke 4:40). 'Jesus cured many who were sick with various diseases, and cast out many demons'. Matthew adds a reference to Isaiah 53:4: 'He took our infirmities and bore our diseases'. People kept bringing the sick to Jesus, for they could feel his empathy, his willingness to share the pain of the sick and their carers. Luke adds: 'He laid his hands on each of them and cured them.' They felt that his touch was personal to 'each of them'. This was central to his mission. He wants each person to know God's personal love. It was Jesus' love and his conviction that God wants people to 'live to the full' (John 10:10) that attracted people to believe in the God whom Jesus revealed and to open their hearts to God's love.

* Jesus' love for a 'leper' (Mark 1:40-45; Matthew 8:1-4; Luke 5:12-14). I have put the word 'leper' in inverted commas. We do not have enough evidence

for an accurate medical diagnosis. He had some form of virulent skin complaint. Whatever it was, it was understood that it was God's will that a person suffering such a complaint had to live outside the community (see Leviticus 13:45-46). They were afraid, for the discoloration of the skin brought them face to face with death. There was something about Jesus that encouraged this man to ignore this regulation, to dare people's rejection, and to approach Jesus: 'If you want to you can make me clean'. Some early manuscripts say that Jesus was 'moved with anger' – presumably at the way people were taught to think that God would want to reject this man. Other manuscripts speak of Jesus being 'moved with compassion'. Leprosy made a person an outsider. Jesus was already having to face rejection, so he knew what it felt like to be an outsider. His response to the man is beautiful: 'Jesus stretched out his hand, touched the man and said: Of course I want to. Be made clean.' To make sure that the man was accepted back into the community, and to his family, Jesus told him to go to the priests whose task it was to judge that he was indeed healed.

* A paralysed man is healed (Mark 2:1-12; Matthew 9:1-8; Luke 5:17-26). Four men bring a friend suffering from paralysis to Jesus. Jesus, as ever, sees to the heart. There is something special about this man's paralysis. His inability to move physically is a symptom of his inability to take steps in his life to renew his relationship with God. It is the man's trust and the obvious love of his friends that invite

Jesus to look below the surface to the source of the paralysis. Jesus never judges us in our sin. He seeks to love us out of it. Jesus wants to help the man find a way to turn from the sin that is paralysing him. When the paralysed man makes space for God to share with him his Spirit, he is free to walk.

* Jesus eats with sinners (Mark 2:15-17; Matthew 9:10-13; Luke 5:29-32). It was the 'sinners' – those who were considered outside the religious community, those forbidden to join the community in the temple or synagogue – who were more open to listen to what Jesus had to say about God. It was the sinners who responded to the good news that God is Love and will never exclude them. Jesus was open to everyone, but it was the 'sinners' who were more open to welcome him. They knew they needed love and they could tell that Jesus, far from rejecting them, loved their company. It was this that opened the way for them to believe they were loved by God.

* Filled with compassion Jesus invites us all: 'Come to me, all you that are weary and are carrying heavy burdens, and I will give you rest. Take my yoke upon you, and learn from me; for I am gentle and humble in heart, and you will find rest for your souls. For my yoke is easy, and my burden is light' (Matthew 11:28-30). No one is meant to be alone. People felt that Jesus was prepared to carry their burdens with them. This led them to reflect on their own experience and to discover the strength to continue their journey, however difficult, in love.

* A man with a withered hand is healed (Mark 3:1-6; Matthew 12:9-14; Luke 6:6-11). Once again we are in the synagogue and it is the Sabbath. There is a man present whose hand is withered. The Pharisees are watching Jesus closely. When the encounter between Jesus and the man leads to a healing, the Pharisees conspire with the followers of Herod 'to destroy him'. They judged Jesus to be thwarting God's revealed will. Jesus wants to free us from being locked into our human traditions: 'for the sake of your tradition, you make void the word of God' (Matthew 15:6). Love must always trump human traditions.

* Jesus and a woman sinner (Luke 7:36-60). Jesus is sitting at table in the house of a Pharisee called Simon. A woman in the city, who was a sinner, having learned that he was eating in the Pharisee's house, brought an alabaster jar of ointment. She stood behind him at his feet, weeping, and began to bathe his feet with her tears and to dry them with her hair. Then she continued kissing his feet and anointing them with the ointment. We can only guess at what experiences have led her to this action. She must have witnessed his words about God and his obvious love and felt impelled to seek him out. Simon and the others at table are astonished that Jesus accepts her behaviour: 'If this man were a prophet, he would have known who and what kind of woman this is who is touching him – that she is a sinner'. In fact, Jesus is the only person there who does know her, because he sees

her love. He does not deny her 'many sins', but he knows that God is love and that where we find love, there we find God. He assures her that her sins must have been forgiven or she could not love so much. Overwhelmed by Jesus' loving response, she finds the peace she is seeking.

* Jesus does not condemn a woman caught in the act of adultery (John 8:3-11). The law, understood as an expression of God's will, is clear: the woman is to be stoned (see Leviticus 20:10). They ask Jesus what they should do with her. If he says they should let her go, they can accuse him of failing to follow God's law. If he says they should stone her, they will have exposed him as a hypocrite. Jesus challenges them: 'Let anyone among you who is without sin be the first to throw a stone at her'. Afraid to face Jesus' penetrating gaze, they slink off, leaving the woman alone with Jesus who assures her that he does not condemn her. He pleads with her not to sin again. The woman, like all of us, is seeking love. Jesus knows that the only way to help her find it is not to condemn her but to offer her love, true love that flows from communion with God and invites us to embrace that communion.

* A deranged man finds peace with Jesus (Mark 5:1-20; Matthew 8:28-34; Luke 8:26-39). He dwells among the tombs, howling and bruising himself with stones. The people had tried to shackle him, but he broke the chains. 'No one had the strength to subdue him.' When he sees Jesus, he has a strange feeling: he feels love. He rushes to Jesus. The people

are amazed to see him there with Jesus 'clothed and in his right mind'. Such is the power of love in one as pure as Jesus.

* A girl is restored to life (Mark 5:22, 40-43; Matthew 9:18, 25; Luke 8:41-42, 54-56). A leader of the synagogue pleads with Jesus to restore his twelve-year-old daughter to life. Jesus takes her by the hand and says to her, 'Talitha cum' ('Little girl, rise up!'). The scenes recorded in the gospels are there for their symbolic power. Here we see that Jesus' love is inviting us to share with him his resurrected life. Death does not have the final word. As we read in the Song of Songs 6:6: 'Set me as a seal upon your heart, as a seal upon your arm; for love is strong as death, passion fierce as the grave. Its flashes are flashes of fire, a raging flame'.

* Jesus' compassion (Mark 6:34; Matthew 14:14 and 9:36). 'Jesus saw the crowd; and he had compassion for them, because they were like sheep without a shepherd; and he began to teach them many things.' It is typical of Mark to focus on Jesus' teaching (Matthew focuses on healing). The people were like sheep without a shepherd because so often the teaching they received about God, and so about life, obscured God's love. This focus on compassion finds expression in two of Jesus' best-known parables.

In the first parable (Luke 10:30-35), Jesus tells a story of a man who is robbed and left half dead on the road from Jerusalem down to Jericho. A priest is riding by, sees him and passes by on the other side. A Levite is walking along the same road and does the same. Then comes a Samaritan The difference is that when the Samaritan sees the man, he is 'moved with compassion', so he pours oil and wine on the man's wounds (something the Levite could have done), then puts him on his animal and takes him to an inn (something the priest could have done). At the inn, he pays the innkeeper to look after him (reversing the violence of the brigands).

The second parable (Luke 15:11-32) is about a man who has two sons. The younger one lives a wasteful life. Then for purely selfish reasons he decides to return to his father's farm, hoping to get a job as a hired worker. 'So he set off and went to his father. But while he was still far off, his father saw him and was filled with compassion; he ran and put his arms around him and kissed him. Then the son said to him: Father, I have sinned against heaven and before you; I am no longer worthy to be called your son.' The boy had planned to ask to be a hired servant. Overwhelmed by the father's compassion, he now wants to be a son. There is no condemnation from the father, only love. 'The father said to his slaves: "Quickly, bring out a robe – the best one – and put it on him; put a ring on his finger and sandals on his feet. Get the fatted calf and kill it, and let us eat and celebrate; for this son of mine was dead and is alive again; he was lost and is found!" And they began to celebrate.'

The focus of the parable moves to the elder son who has dutifully stayed home and worked the farm. When he finds out that the father has welcomed the boy home he is angry, and refuses to join the celebration even though the father pleads with him: 'Son, you are always with me, and all that is mine is yours. But we had to celebrate and rejoice, because this brother of yours was dead and has come to life; he was lost and has been found'. Jesus pleads with us: 'Be merciful just as your Father is merciful' (Luke 6:36). The father in this parable offers us a beautiful picture of God as Jesus knew God to be: a God of compassion whose delight is to celebrate life with us, whatever our situation.

* 'I am the good shepherd. I know my own and my own know me, just as the Father knows me and I know the Father. And I lay down my life for my sheep' (John 10:14). Jesus gives himself to us in love, inviting us to see the whole universe and ourselves as God's Self-gift in love.

* 'He will not break a bruised reed or quench a smouldering wick' (Matthew 12:20).

* Jesus learns through the love and faith of a woman from Tyre who pleads with him to heal her daughter (Mark 7:24-30; Matthew 15:21-28). Jesus was always responsive to God's call. In Matthew's version, Jesus understands that his Father's will is for him to minister to Israelites. Through this woman's obvious love and persistent trust in God, Jesus comes to see that God is calling him to reveal God also to the Gentiles.

* An epileptic boy finds healing (Mark 9:14-29; Matthew 17:14-20; Luke 9:37-43). A distraught father brings his tortured boy to Jesus and describes the boy's convulsions. Jesus says to him: 'All things can be done for the one who believes'. The father responds: 'I believe; help my unbelief'. Then Jesus takes the boy by the hand and lifts him up, and he is able to stand. When the disciples ask Jesus why they were unable to help, Jesus tells them of the importance of prayer. Jesus draws his love from his

communion with his Father. It must be the same for us.

* Jesus looks on a man with love (Mark 10:17-22; Matthew 19:16-26; Luke 18:18-28). We have been watching scenes from Jesus' life. We have been observing the effects on people of Jesus' love. Mark draws our attention to a man who is rich but who knows there must be more to life than possessions. He cannot help noticing the deep communion that exists between Jesus and his disciples, and he wants to know what he has to do to share it. Jesus refers him to God's commandments. The man assures Jesus: 'I have kept all these from my youth'. Then 'Jesus, looking at him, loved him'. He invites him to unclutter his life by sharing his possessions with the poor, then 'come, follow me.' Tragically, 'the man went away grieving'. In the depths of his soul he knew what he wanted, and he knew that he would find it by joining Jesus' disciples, but he was not ready to leave the life to which he had become accustomed. Imagine the sadness of Jesus when the man walked off. Jesus loves me and offers me the challenge to let go of whatever it is that is holding me back from following my deepest longings. What is my response?

* A blind man has his sight restored (Mark 10:46-52; Matthew 20:29-34; Luke 18:35-43). A blind beggar is sitting by the side of the road. He is told that Jesus is passing that way, and persistently cries out for mercy. Jesus hears his cry and arranges for people to bring the man to him. With profound respect,

Jesus asks him: 'What do you want me to do for you?' Encouraged by Jesus' love the man asks to see again. Jesus assures him: 'Your faith has made you well'. The man sees. Such is Jesus' attraction that he 'followed Jesus on the way'. The gospel-writers see this man as symbolic of a disciple. Having been 'enlightened', we are all called to follow Jesus to Jerusalem, to Calvary, and to the Resurrection.

* At the Last Supper (Mark 14:22-24; Matthew 26:26-28; Luke 22:19-20), Jesus promises to be with his disciples after his death: 'I will come again and take you to myself, so that where I am there you may be also' (John 14:3). Every time we come together and eat the Eucharistic bread, he will give himself to us in love to nourish us. Every time we come together to drink the Eucharistic wine, he will pour into our thirsty hearts his life that is about to be poured from his heart on Calvary.

* Jesus looks at Peter (Luke 22:61). We have already reflected on the love that is communicated by Jesus' look. Here we see it again. Peter is bewildered by what is happening to Jesus. He manages to get into the courtyard of the house of the high priest, but when he is challenged he denies he even knows Jesus. Luke's version continues: 'The LORD turned and looked at Peter': a look of sadness no doubt, but a look of forgiveness and love; a look that had a profound effect on Peter who 'went out and wept bitterly'.

* Jesus offers all his love to a man crucified with him (Luke 23:39-43). One of the men crucified with

Jesus senses something special in him, and pleads with him: 'Jesus, remember me when you come into your kingdom'. From his heart filled as always with love Jesus responds: 'Truly I tell you, today you will be with me in Paradise'.

We have been watching Jesus love. Let us focus now on what this means for us

Having invited anyone who is thirsty to come to him and drink, Jesus promises: 'Out of his heart will flow rivers of living water' (John 7:38). Out of Jesus' heart, yes, but also out of the disciple's heart, for in giving us his Spirit, in giving us the love he experiences with his Father, Jesus is giving us what he promised the woman at the well: 'the water I will give will become in you a spring of water gushing up to eternal life' (John 4:14). Jesus invites us to follow him in loving because he knows that we can share with him in the love he receives from the Father. He knows that if we draw on the source that sustains him, we can learn to love as he loves. We can learn to love with the love he is giving us.

At the Last Supper, Jesus speaks of himself as a vine and of us as his branches (John 15:5). We have been watching the love that the vine produces. He wants us to go on bearing the fruit of love: 'I give you a new commandment, that you love one another. Just as I have loved you, you also should love one another' (John 13:34). He is not asking us to love like him. He wants us to allow him to love through us. He even declares: 'Very truly, I tell you, the one who believes in me will also do the works that I do and, in fact, will do greater works than these, because I am going to the Father' (John 14:12). Prior to his death, Jesus' ability to love was necessarily limited by time and place. Now, from his communion in love with God, he can pour out his Spirit of love into the hearts of anyone who is willing to love with his love.

'Father, as you have sent me into the world, so I have sent them into the world' (John 17:18). It is through the love we show people that they experience Jesus' love and realise that it comes from God and that God loves them even as God loves Jesus (John 17:23). Jesus prays that people will come to see that 'the love with which you, Father, have loved me may be in them, and I in them' (John 17:26). We choose to *be-lieve*: we choose to *be* in his *love*. This encourages others to do the same. 'Beloved, let us love one another, because love is from God' (1 John 4:7). 'No one has ever seen God. If we love one another, God lives in us and God's love is perfected in us' (1 John 4:12). 'God is love. If you abide in love, you abide in God, and God abides in you' (1 John 4:16). It is God's love that fills the heart of Jesus, and he wants us to open our hearts to welcome this love.

In what may be Paul's earliest extant letter, he states: 'God was pleased to reveal his Son in me, so that I might proclaim him among the Gentiles' (Galatians 1:16). When people looked at Paul, they saw Jesus, and in seeing Jesus they were seeing God. Paul opened his heart so totally to welcome the love that Jesus was giving him that he could say: 'It is no longer I who live. It is Christ who lives in me. The life I now live in the flesh I live by the faith of the Son of God, loving me and giving himself for me' (Galatians 2:20). Jesus believes in God as love and shares this belief with Paul. 'God has sent the Spirit of his Son into our hearts, crying "Abba! Father"' (Galatians 4:6). The first fruit of the Spirit is love (Galatians 5:22). Paul is speaking of divine love in the human heart of Jesus. It is this love that Jesus shares with us who are 'the glorious possession of our LORD Jesus, the Messiah (2 Thessalonians 2:14).

Paul reminds the community in Corinth that they are 'God's temple and God's Spirit dwells in you' (1 Corinthians 3:16). He is speaking of the Spirit of love that flows between the heart of Jesus and the heart of God. We can love with Jesus' love because 'anyone united to the LORD becomes one Spirit with him' (1 Corinthians 6:17). We are called to love, each of us uniquely according to the way in which Jesus lives in us: 'To each is given the manifestation of the Spirit for a good purpose' (1 Corinthians 12:7). The 'good purpose' is, of course, love. From his prayer-communion with Jesus and from his belonging in the Christian community, Paul speaks of love: 'Love never stops caring. Love acts always in a kind way. Love does not act out of jealousy or envy. Love does not boast; or behave arrogantly. Love does not behave indecently or insist on its own way. Love does not give way to irritation; or brood over wrongs. Love takes no pleasure in wrongdoing, but rejoices in the truth. Love has space enough to hold and to bear everything and everyone. Love believes all things, hopes all things, and endures whatever comes. Love does not come to an end' (1 Corinthians 13:4-8).

Because it is Jesus' love that we are graced to share, 'we are the aroma of Christ to God' (2 Corinthians 2:15). God welcomes our love. It is ours, yes; but it is the love Jesus gives us, the love God shares with Jesus his Son. When other people experience our love, they are experiencing the love of God shining on the face and in the heart of Jesus: 'God has shone in our hearts to give the light of the knowledge of the glory of God on the face of Jesus, the Messiah' (2 Corinthians 4:6).

We are called and graced to love one another with Jesus' love. This is possible because 'God has given Christ who is head of all things to the church which is his body, the fullness of him who is in everything and fills everything' (Ephesians 1:22-23).

The Risen Jesus wants to fill our hearts, for us, and so that he can love others in us and through us: 'I pray that Christ may dwell in your hearts through faith as you are being rooted and grounded in love' (Ephesians 3:16-17). 'We must grow up in every way into him ... building up the body in love' (Ephesians 4:16). 'Be imitators of God, as beloved children, and live in love, as Christ loved us and gave himself up for us' (Ephesians 5:1-2).

Paul had a special love for the community in Philippi. He knew that he was not the source of this love: 'I long for you all with the compassion of the Messiah Jesus' (Philippians 1:8). 'To me living is the Messiah (Philippians 1:21). 'If there is any appeal in the Messiah, any consolation from love, any communion in the Spirit, any movements of compassion and feelings of love, make my joy complete by being of the same mind, being of one soul and of one mind ... Let the same mind be in you that was in the Messiah Jesus' (Philippians 2:1-2, 5).

CHAPTER SIX

JESUS THE WORD OF GOD MADE FLESH

When the scriptures speak of the 'Word of God', they are speaking of God as giving expression to God's will, to God's Self-revelation. In the dramatic account in the Book of Genesis, it is the Word of God that brings creation into existence, beginning with the command: 'Let there be light' (Genesis 1:3). This is the Word of which Isaiah speaks: 'The Word that goes from my mouth does not return to me empty, without carrying out my will and succeeding in what it was sent to do' (Isaiah 55:11).

There is a close link between God's Wisdom and God's Word. The Wisdom of God is God as reflected in the beauty and order of creation, of history, of the Torah, and of Jesus. The Word of God is God as the sustaining cause of this beauty and this order. This theme is taken up in the opening verses of the Letter to the Hebrews: 'At various times in the past and in various different ways, God spoke to our ancestors through the prophets; but in our own time, the last days, God has spoken to us through God's Son, the Son that God has appointed to inherit everything and through whom God made everything there is' (Hebrews 1:1-2).

The scriptures speak of 'God's Wisdom', 'God's Presence', 'God's Spirit', 'God's Word'. When they personify the Wisdom of

God, the Spirit of God, the Word of God, they are expressing their profound faith in the presence of God in their lives. God's Wisdom is God as wise. In the same way, God's Word is God as declaring God's will and communicating God's being. We find, for example, in the Book of Wisdom: 'When peaceful silence lay over all, and night had run the half of her swift course, down from the heavens, from the royal throne, leapt your all-powerful Word carrying your command like a sharp sword' (Wisdom 18:14-15).

In the Prologue to his Gospel the Beloved Disciple personifies the 'Word' of God. Then in verse fourteen, he speaks of Jesus as the human embodiment of the divine Word. This is brought out more clearly if, instead of translating the Greek pronoun with 'he', we repeat the noun 'Word'. In the following translation of the Prologue, each time the noun *'Word'* is used where the Greek has a pronoun, it is italicised.

> In the beginning was the Word and the Word was towards God and the Word was God. *The Word* was towards God in the beginning. By means of *the Word* all things came to be and nothing has come to be without *the Word*. That which came to be in *the Word* was life and that life was the light of humankind, a light that shines in the dark, a light that darkness could not overpower. (John 1:1-5)

We are taken back to the dawn of creation when God summoned creation into being, when light dispelled the darkness of primordial chaos. Creation reflected God and from the heart of creation a Word was addressed back to God. A dialogue was begun between God and creation. Creation experienced itself facing towards God, and drawn towards God as its goal.

The Word was the true light, which, coming into the world, enlightens all humankind. *The Word* was in the world and the world came into being by means of *the Word*, yet the world did not know *the Word*. *The Word* came to *the Word's* own domain and *the Word's* own people did not receive *the Word*. But to all who did receive *the Word the Word* gave power to become children of God. All who believe in the name of *the Word* were born not of human stock, nor of earthly desire, nor of human will, but of God. And the Word became flesh and dwelt among us, and we beheld the glory of *the Word* full of grace and truth' (John 1:9-14).

The Word of God that found expression in creation and in history, in the Law (the Torah) and in the Prophets, the Word of God that was largely unheeded and rejected, finally 'became flesh'. God's Word is revealed in the flesh of the man Jesus of Nazareth. It was he who revealed to the Beloved Disciple and his contemporaries what God's Word had been revealing since the beginning of creation. The Word of God had sought a place in which to dwell, and had pitched a tent in Israel. Now, finally, the Word found a home in human flesh. This was the man Jesus whom the Beloved Disciple had known. The Glory of God could be seen in creation, in history, and in Israel. God was revealed in a human way in the flesh of Jesus of Nazareth. 'And we beheld him.' The Beloved Disciple experienced Jesus' love and came to believe that Jesus is full of God's love. Jesus is the one who speaks God's words of love to us, who takes us into the very heart of God, and reveals the covenant of love offered by God from the beginning. He reveals the faithfulness of God. He shows us the truth of God, revealing what God really is.

> From his fullness we have all received, yes, grace upon grace. The Law was given through Moses, grace and truth came through Jesus the Messiah. No one has ever seen God. The only-begotten Son who is in the bosom of the Father has made God known.
> (John 1:16-18)

The conclusion brings the reader to the revelation of God that Jesus gave and continues to give us. It prepares us for the Gospel in which Jesus gives this revelation, first in many signs, and finally when he is lifted up on the cross. This hymn to the Word expresses the main theme of the Gospel of the Beloved Disciple: Jesus is God's Word to us. Jesus is the revelation of God. The final verse leaves the reader with a picture of special intimacy. Just as the Beloved Disciple reclined in Jesus' bosom, so Jesus is 'in the bosom of the Father', resting against God's heart, in intimate communion, learning secrets never before revealed. It is Jesus who 'has made God known'.

Furthermore, however splendid was the gracious gift God gave us when God revealed God's will to us through Moses, this is but the background against which the revelation given in Jesus stands out in magnificent relief. In Jesus we see God's *hesed we 'emet* ('grace and truth'), God's covenant love and fidelity. Jesus reveals the very being of God.

The hymn focuses our attention on the man Jesus in the weakness of his mortal state (in the 'flesh'). It is in his human frailty – in fact, as the Beloved Disciple mentions again and again, in his life-giving on the cross – that he reveals to us the radiant beauty of God.

A good commentary on the Prologue is the First Letter composed within the community of the Beloved Disciple: 'Something which has existed since the beginning, that we have heard, and we have seen with our own eyes; that we have watched and touched with our hands: the Word, who is life – this is our subject. That life was made visible: we saw it and we are giving our testimony, telling you of the eternal life which was with the Father and has been made visible to us' (1 John 1:1-4).

Jesus, the man known to the Beloved Disciple, is the incarnation, the realisation of God in our human condition, the human embodiment of God who has been communicating God's Self through creation and through the history of Israel.

If we wish to see who Jesus is, we must start where his disciples started: with a human being. It is when, like the disciples, we watch him in prayer that we see and are drawn into his divinity, his intimate communion with God. To see God revealed we must 'look on the one whom they have pierced' (John 19:37). Jesus, who is the Word of God made flesh, is indeed 'flesh'. And he manifests the Glory of God, he reveals God's Wisdom, and he speaks God's Word of love, when he is lifted up on the cross. We are to watch him there to see revealed, not just the faithful love of a wonderful man. We are to see revealed there God's Wisdom; we are to hear there, clearly spoken, God's Word. Enlightened by those who knew and loved him, our gaze focuses on Jesus who enlightens, loves, liberates and saves the world. The way to come to know God who speaks God's Word, is to contemplate Jesus, the Word who is spoken: 'This is my Son, the Beloved; listen to him' (Mark 9:7).

CHAPTER SEVEN

JESUS' TEACHING ABOUT OUR RESPONSE TO GOD

In Chapter One and again in Chapter Four, we contemplated Jesus, the Son, living out his response to God his Father. Here, I would like to concentrate more closely on this aspect of his person, and, at the same time, to listen to his teaching on the response to God that he encouraged in others. In this way, we can hope to come to a deeper appreciation of what it meant for him to be the Son of God, as well as acquire a more accurate understanding of Jesus' vision of what we are called to be.

Jesus was convinced that God was the Father of all, and so his heart went out to everyone without exception and his teaching was addressed to 'anyone who has ears to hear' (Mark 4:9).

At the same time, it is clear from the Gospels that Jesus saw himself as having a special mission to the poor. We have already noted that on a visit to his hometown he chose to preach on a text from Isaiah, which began: 'The spirit of the LORD has been given to me, for he has appointed me. He has sent me to bring the good news to the poor' (Luke 4:18 = Isaiah 61:1). The text goes on to give examples of the poor: the captives, the blind, and the downtrodden. The same picture emerges from the beatitudes. The first reads: 'How blessed and happy are you who are poor: yours is the kingdom of heaven' (Luke 6:20; Matthew 5:3). The poor are described as those who are hungry, who weep, who are hated, driven out, abused and denounced. Elsewhere, Jesus gives as examples 'the crippled, the blind and the lame' (Luke 14:13, 21).

This is consistent with the meaning of 'poor' that is found throughout the Bible, as can be seen from the following oracle from the prophet Amos: 'For the crimes of Israel I have made my decree and will not relent: because they have sold the virtuous for silver and the poor (*'ebion*) for a pair of sandals, because they trample on the heads of ordinary people and push the poor (*'anawim*) out of their path' (Amos 2:6-7). *'ebion* and *'anaw* are the words used most frequently in the Hebrew scriptures for the poor.

'ebion focuses on the ideas of need and powerlessness. The image is that of a beggar, arms outstretched, utterly dependent on others for what he needs, unable to cope on his own; the redundant person, the lonely person, the person without a voice, the last in the line; the hungry person, the thirsty, the blind, the deaf, the paralysed. The word has nothing to do with imaginary 'needs', distracting desires, superficial, self-inflicted frustrations. It is referring to basic human needs that are required for life itself. The *'ebion*, the poor, cannot supply these basic needs for themselves, but have to rely on others for them.

'anaw accents the idea of oppression. The image is of a person who is stooped, burdened by other people's unjust oppression. The *'anawim* are the downtrodden, the deserted, the deprived, the outcast, the cast aside, the despised, the humiliated, the roughly-treated, the yoked, the trapped, the captive, crushed by the blows of misery. It adds to the idea of *'ebion* the fact that the poor are in need because of other

people's actions in their regard.

Jesus understood that he had a special mission to the *'ebion* and the *'anawim*, to those in need and to the oppressed. This was not because there was some special merit in being in need or in being oppressed; nor was it because the poor, by virtue of their poverty, necessarily had some special quality that made them fit to receive and enjoy the good news. When Jesus said 'How blessed and happy are you who are poor' (Luke 6:20), he was not admiring them in their poverty, or holding them up as examples, he was assuring them that God was determined to redeem them from their poverty. The hungry were about to be satisfied, the weeping were about to laugh (Luke 6:21), the blind were about to see again, the lame to walk, the lepers to be cleansed, the deaf to hear and the dead to be raised to life (Matthew 11:5; Luke 7:22). The good news was that God was about to reign, and God would meet their needs and take away their oppression, as God had done for their ancestors in Egypt.

There are many ways of being in need, and there are many forms of oppression. The heart of Jesus went out to them all, offering them release. The greatest need of all was the need to be loved, and Jesus offered that to each. With love came a challenge that varied according to each one's need. To some, the challenge was to unclutter themselves from the material possessions that were stifling their spirit. We see Zacchaeus, 'one of the senior tax collectors and a wealthy man' (Luke 19:2) accepting Jesus' challenge and welcoming Jesus and the good news with joy. On the other hand, we read of another man 'of great wealth' (Mark 10:22; Matthew 19:22; Luke 18:23) who had a deep longing for life and who approached Jesus begging for help. Jesus, we are told, 'looked steadily at him and loved him' (Mark 10:21). He invited him to come with him, and told him to unburden himself of his wealth and give it to those who needed it. This man was unable to accept the challenge and 'went away sad' (Mark 10:22). For others, the challenge was to let go their pride, whether based on learning, or reputation, or position in society. We see Nicodemus attempting to meet this challenge (John 3:1-21) by coming to the light (John 3:21). We see many others going away empty from Jesus' love and from the challenge of the good news (Luke 1:53), unrepentant (Luke 3:8), unforgiven (Luke 18:9-14). Jesus himself declared: 'All those who exalt themselves will be humbled. Those who humble themselves will be exalted' (Luke 14:11, 18:14). For others, the challenge was to stop worrying, to cease being preoccupied with distractions (Luke 11:38-42).

Each person has to make their own journey in response to Jesus' love and to the good news he preached. There are obvious material and psychological needs that cause us to classify certain people as being in need (*'ebion*). There are certain obvious oppressions that cause us to classify people as being among the '*anawim*. Jesus recognised that our most profound need is for love, for God's love. He saw that our greatest oppression is to be deprived of love. The leper suffered from this in one way, Zacchaeus in another. Jesus' heart went out to all. His mission was to all. He challenged us to take whatever steps are appropriate to open ourselves to God's love.

Jesus' universal mission was limited by the fact that his ministry lasted only two or three years. He had little opportunity to go outside Galilee and Judea. Another limitation was from people's response to him. It seems that those whose needs were greatest, since they were trapped in their own pride and possessions, were most resistant to Jesus' message and offer of love, whereas those whose needs were more humiliating, being harder to hide, were those who responded to Jesus' offer and sought his company (Luke 15:1). So we find Jesus sharing table-fellowship with people of all classes of society, but his reputation was for 'eating with sinners and tax collectors' (Mark 2:16). We find him preaching and reaching out in love to people of all conditions, but in fact surrounded by the outcasts of society.

This was not simply the result of people's response to him, though this no doubt played a large part in what happened. Jesus did not just wait around and remain available! He had a mission from God, and he purposely chose to be with those in need. He chose to take the side of the oppressed.

Jesus' conviction that God did indeed want to save those in need and those suffering oppression was based on his own personal experience. He experienced need himself, and suffered oppression, and he experienced the love of his Father meeting his need and liberating him from oppression. His teaching was a matter of inviting others to share his own experience of the love of his Father.

From what we have already noted, it is obvious that there is no automatic connection between being poor and experiencing the blessing of God. Need and oppression can lead to greed, violence and despair. In holding out hope for the poor, Jesus also taught us the kind of response that is necessary from us if we are to enjoy relief and experience redemption. The effectiveness of his mission was essentially related to people's response, for he offered them love, and they were free to accept or reject the offer.

The essence of Jesus' teaching was that the poor were to recognise that God is their Father, and so learn to respond to God as children. Jesus himself, as we have seen, related as Son; he called for the same response from others: 'I tell you solemnly, anyone who does not welcome the kingdom of God like a little child will never enter it' (Mark 10:15; Matthew 18:3;

Luke 18:17). Let us examine the response of a child under three aspects: children cry out to their father when in distress; children listen to their father and obey him; children place their trust in their father's love and believe in him. This was how Jesus responded to God; it was the advice he gave to others.

In our distress we are invited to call on God.

By definition, the poor cannot satisfy their own need, nor can they rid themselves of the yoke of oppression. What else can they do but cry out for relief? This is what Jesus did throughout his life (see Hebrews 5:7), but notably in his final hours. Mark describes the scene in Gethsemane.

> Jesus took Peter and James and John with him. And a sudden fear came over him, and great distress. And he said to them: my soul is sorrowful to the point of death. Wait here, and keep awake. And going on a little further he threw himself on the ground and prayed that, if it were possible, this hour might pass him by: 'Abba (Father)!' he said. 'Everything is possible for you. Take this cup away from me. But let it be as you, not I, would have it' (Mark 14:33-36; Matthew 26:37-39; Luke 22:41-42; compare John 12:27).

We find the same cry rising to the Father from Jesus in his dying moments. Mark (15:34) and Matthew (27:46) place on his lips the first words of Psalm 22, in this way inviting the reader to pray this psalm as a way of reflecting on the way in which Jesus suffered, cried out to God, and accepted his final agony. Let us accept their invitation here, for a reading of Psalm 22 does give us a profound insight into Jesus' heart and mind at the end of his life; it also expresses powerfully the attitude he tried to inculcate in the poor.

> My God, my God, why have you deserted me?
> How far from saving me, the words I groan!
> I call all day, my God, but you never answer,
>   all night long I call and cannot rest. (Psalm 22:1-2).

The 'poor of YHWH' are those who call to God in their distress. We are encouraged to call because of the fidelity of YHWH in the past:

> Yet, Holy One, you who make your home in the praises
>   of Israel,
> in you our ancestors put their trust, they trusted and
>   you rescued them;
> they called to you for help and they were saved,
> they never trusted you in vain. (Psalm 22:3-5).

Sustained by faith, the poor remind God of God's personal promise to them and of the care God offered them in times past.

> Yet here am I, now more worm than human being,
> scorn of humanity, jest of the people,
> all who see me jeer at me, they toss their heads and
>   sneer:
> He relied on God, let God save him! If God is his friend,
>   let God rescue him!
> Yet you drew me out of the womb, you entrusted me to
>   my mother's breasts;
> placed on your lap from my birth, from my mother's
>   womb you have been my God,

> Do not stand aside. Trouble is near. I have no one to help me!' (Psalm 22:6-11).

The poor man goes on to describe his condition with phrases like:

> 'I am like water draining away, my bones are all disjointed,
> my heart is like wax, melting inside me ...
> they tie me hand and foot and leave me lying in the dust of death' (Psalm 22:12-18).

He concludes his plea with a final cry and a promise to praise God:

> 'Do not stand aside, YHWH. O my strength, come quickly to my help...
> Then I shall proclaim your name to my brothers, praise you in full assembly' (Psalm 22:19-22).

God, the redeemer, hears the cry of the poor, who cries out in exultation:

> 'You who fear YHWH, praise him! Entire race of Jacob, glorify him!
> Entire race of Israel, revere him!
> For God has not despised or disdained the poor one in his poverty,
> has not hidden God's face, but has answered when he called'
> (Psalm 22:23-24).

What we contemplate when we watch Jesus is what we hear when we listen to his teaching. He tells the poor to cry to God for their 'daily bread' (Matthew 6:11; Luke 11:3). He tells them to pray to God to keep them safe in the time of destruction that was imminent (Matthew 6: I 3; Luke 11:4). He tells them: 'Ask, and it will be given to you; search, and you will find; knock, and the door will be opened to you. For whoever asks always receives; whoever searches always finds; whoever knocks will always have the door opened to them' (Matthew 7:7-8; Luke 11:9-11; also Mark 11:24; Matthew 21:22; John 16:24; Matthew 18:19-20). Jesus concluded his story about the persistent widow with the words: 'Will not God see justice done to his chosen who cry to God day and night, even when God delays to help them?' (Luke 18:7).

We are to listen to God and follow God's inspiration.

There is no point in crying to God if we fail to listen to God and respond to God's inspiration. God does want to answer our need and release us from oppression. As children of God, we must be 'obedient'. Note the Latin roots of the word obedience: 'ob-audiens' = close listening in response to the call of another. The Hebrew and Greek words for 'obedience' also derive from words meaning 'listen'.

Jesus hungered for every word that came from his Father (Matthew 4:4). He said once: 'My food is to do the will of the One who sent me' (John 4:34; see also John 5:30, 6:38, 7:28-29, 12:48-49). The Letter to the Hebrews says of him: 'Although he was Son, he learned to obey through suffering' (Hebrews 5:8). His cry of agony in Gethsemane is followed by the words: 'Let it be as you, Father, not I, would have it' (Mark 14:36). This is the attitude one would expect from a son towards his father. It is an attitude that characterises Jesus, and an attitude that he tries to inculcate in the poor: 'It is not those who say to me,

"LORD, LORD," who will enter the kingdom of heaven, but the person who does the will of my Father' (Matthew 7:21). 'Anyone who does the will of God, that person is my brother and sister and mother' (Mark 3:35; Matthew 12:50; Luke 8:21).

The obedience that Jesus lived and taught was not a blind resignation to fate or destiny, as though we are puppets in the hands of an autocratic deity. It is an obedience that comes from a free heart (John 10:18) that trusts in the wisdom of God's will, offering us the way to salvation and freedom. It is an obedience that requires all our courage and creativity, qualities possible only if we trust that God is indeed our Father.

Jesus' constant and faithful attention to the will of his Father drew him into his mission of love. In spite of the sinful intransigence of his opponents, he sustained this love even when it was taking him on a course that led to the cross. Jesus kept obeying his Father, because he knew that if obeying in love meant his dying, somehow God would use this death to save and liberate. He also knew that God would 'save him out of death' (Hebrews 5:7). In other words, both the crying out to God, and the attentive listening to God, are expressions of the fundamental attitude of a child to a father: an attitude of trust.

We must keep believing in God.

Jesus' trust in God his Father is evident throughout the Gospels. As he journeys through the desert of this world, and leads others along the way, he shows them how to believe; how to 'be' in the 'love' of God their Father, and how to remain in that love (see Hebrews 2:13, 12:2). Even when he is faced with death, he keeps believing that his Father will be faithful to him, and will raise him, through death, into glory (Mark 8:31;

Matthew 16:21; Luke 9:22; Mark 9:31; Matthew 17:23; and Mark 10:34; Matthew 20:19; Luke 18:33; Luke 13:32).

Jesus encourages this same attitude in others. What do the poor have to offer except their humble readiness to receive? Only such an attitude would open them to God's gracious Spirit, and so to the power to be able to listen to God and carry out God's will (see Romans 3:21-22). 'Everything is possible', says Jesus, 'to a person who has faith' (Mark 9:23). He tells us not to worry about food or clothing or length of life (Matthew 6:25-34; Luke 12:22-31). He tells us not to worry even about persecution (Mark 13:11; Matthew 10:18-20; Luke 21:14-15). He tells us never to be afraid of God, for God cares for us far more than any father on earth, even to numbering the hairs on our head (Matthew 10:30; Luke 12:7). Jesus encourages us: 'Do not let your hearts he troubled. Trust in God still, and trust in me' (John 14:1).

Mark summarises the preaching of Jesus in the command: 'Believe in the good news' (Mark 1:15). Jesus' heart rejoices at the healing that flowed through him from his Father to those who did believe: those like the paralysed man (Mark 2:5; Matthew 9:2; Luke 5:20), the woman with a haemorrhage (Mark 5:34; Matthew 9:22; Luke 8:48), and the blind man (Mark 10:52; Luke 18:42). Jesus encourages Jairus to 'have faith' and God would answer his prayer (Mark 5:36; Luke 8:50). When Peter was disturbed by the withering of the fig tree and the emptying of the temple, and was wondering what to build his life on, Jesus tells him: 'Have faith in God' (Mark 11:22; Matthew 21:21). He questions his disciples when they lose heart during the storm: 'How is it that you have no faith?' (Mark 4:40; Matthew 8:26; Luke 8:25). It is her faith that opens the poor lost woman to God's healing forgiveness (Luke 7:50). It is the same with the leper (Luke 17:19).

Jesus is our 'leader in faith' (Hebrews 12:2). When we are being loved, and open ourselves to that love, and respond in love, a whole new world opens up before us. Faith opens us to insights we could never have without it, and it makes things possible that, without faith, are not possible. When people place their trust in Jesus' love, and recognise the religious dimension of his love, and so open themselves to believe in God's love because of him, all kinds of marvellous things become possible. No wonder Jesus prayed that, whatever might happen to Peter, his faith would not fail (Luke 22:32). No wonder he pleaded with Thomas: 'Doubt no longer, but believe' (John 20:27).

There is a beautiful statement of faith in the final verses of the prophecy of Habakkuk:

> Even though the fig tree does not blossom, and there is no fruit on the vine;
> even though the yield of the olive fails, and the fields afford no food;
> even though the sheep vanish from the fold, and there are no cattle in the stalls;
> I will rejoice in YHWH, I will exult in God my Saviour.
> YHWH my LORD is my strength, who makes my feet as light as a doe's,
> and sets my steps on the heights. (Habakkuk 3:17-19).

Such was the exultation of Mary, Jesus' mother, who was blessed by God and who 'believed that the promise made to her by the LORD would be fulfilled' (Luke 1:45). Such was the trust manifested by Jesus himself as he hung upon the cross. Such was the basic attitude encouraged by Jesus in the poor. He not only encouraged this attitude in them, he also made it possible by his own faith, and by the love with which he met them, witnessing as he did to the love of God.

It was this basic attitude of faith that Jesus' disciples knew to be at the heart of their response to the good news: 'We ourselves have known and put our faith in God's love towards ourselves. God is love and those who live in love live in God, and God lives in them' (1 John 4:16).

Faith is essentially something of the heart. Hence the warning given by Jesus: 'Where your treasure is, there will your heart be also. The lamp of the body is the eye. It follows that if your eye is sound, your whole body will be filled with light. But if your eye is diseased, your whole body will be all darkness. If, then, the light inside you is darkness, what darkness that will be ... Set your hearts on the kingdom of your Father first, and on his righteousness, and all these other things will be given you as well' (Matthew 6:21-23, 33).

There are many things that can block our vision, or distract us, and so seduce our heart. Jesus revealed the good news of God's saving love. He taught those in need and those who were oppressed to recognise their total dependence on love – the love that is constantly offered them by God their Father as a free gift. He taught the poor not to seek relief in riches, but to see everything as a gift of love, to be enjoyed as a gift, and to be shared with those in need. He taught them that 'what matters is faith that makes its power felt through love' (Galatians 5:6). This is the bliss that he promised the poor (Matthew 5:3; Luke 6:20).

There is nothing mean, nothing small, nothing frightened or negative about the response asked of us. It is whole-hearted and broad-minded. The horizon opened up for us by the good news is as large as life, as comprehensive as the world. The reign of God is for all. At the same time, the focus is sharp:

our hope is to be in God alone. God hears our cry, and we must listen for God's response. The poor who listen to the teaching of Jesus will accept and live out their total dependence on Love.

Jesus invites the poor to join him in being instruments of God's healing, saving and redeeming love to others. Our greatest poverty is our inability to love. Jesus invites us to love as he loves. He gives us his love to make this possible. Jesus' disciples, like himself, would have to live within the confines of place, time, opportunity, and acceptance or rejection. At the same time, Jesus challenges us not to stand by and wait, but to go out and meet the poor in their need, by giving bread to the hungry, drink to the thirsty, making a stranger welcome, clothing the naked, visiting the sick and the prisoner (see Matthew 26:35-36). As his disciples, we are to wait, but not for the hungry to come to us. We are to wait on God's love filling our hearts and moving us to be instruments of God's healing and liberating Spirit.

Jesus invites us to join in his mission of convincing people that their deepest need is for love, and that the love they need is being offered to them by God. This universal aspect of Jesus' mission is of its essence: 'Come to me all you who labour and are overburdened, and I will give you rest' (Matthew 11:28).

Our world is labouring and overburdened. Our world is seeking rest. We are desperately hoping for good news, especially the good news that our deepest need, our need for love, has an answer. The answer trumpeted forth by many has to do with possessions, as though they could fill our need. We are encouraged to be independent, to be self-made, self-reliant, self-centred. Such directions lead only to isolation, loneliness and alienation. The teaching of Jesus challenges and enlightens us. He invites us to know that we all have the one Father, who hears our cry, knows our need, and is answering us. He invites us to be children of this Father, and so in our relations with each other to learn to be mutually interdependent; in other words, to love.

Those who listened to Jesus formed communities in which spiritual and material riches were shared with the object of meeting everyone's needs in love. These communities were open to all, without regard to racial, religious or economic background (Acts 2:44-45; Galatians 3:28; Ephesians 4:16), and the catholic (universal) nature of their response has characterised authentic Christianity ever since.

There is an urgent need again in our times for disciples of Jesus to work out ways of sharing their spiritual and material gifts in ways appropriate to today's conditions, for only a community organised in love to bring the good news to the poor can claim to be a community that is following Jesus.

In the ultimate analysis we are all poor, in that we are all totally dependent on love for our existence. A tragedy occurs when we do not recognise our need, or, having recognised it, seek to meet it in distracting ways. Jesus, the Son of God, teaches us that the only hope we have is in God, and that our basic response is to be that of a child, a response of trust.

* We are to 'be merciful just as your Father is merciful' (Luke 6:36).

* We are to do all that we can that people will 'live and live to the full' (John 10:10). This is dramatically portrayed in Jesus giving life to a widow's only son (Luke 7:11-15), to Jairus' daughter (Luke 8:54-55), and to Lazarus (John 11:43-44).

* Jesus tells us to 'let your light shine before others, so that they may see your good words and give glory to your Father in heaven' (Matthew 5:16).

* 'You have heard that it was said, "An eye for an eye and a tooth for a tooth". But I say to you: Do not resist an evildoer. If anyone strikes you on the right cheek, turn the other also; and if anyone wants to sue you and take your coat, give your cloak as well; and if anyone forces you to go one mile, go also the second mile. Give to everyone who begs from you, and do not refuse anyone who wants to borrow from you' (Matthew 5:38-42).

* When chaos is threatening us, we are to listen to Jesus and keep our eyes on him. Jesus demonstrates that nothing can separate us from God's love. If we listen for his call and if we keep our eyes on him, we can, like him, 'walk on water'. Peter witnesses to this: 'LORD, if it is you, command me to come to you on the water.' Jesus said, 'Come'. So Peter got out of the boat, started walking on the water, and came toward Jesus. But when he noticed the strong wind, he became frightened, and beginning to sink, he cried out, 'LORD, save me!' Jesus immediately reached out his hand and caught him, saying to him, 'You of little faith, why did you doubt?' (Matthew 14:28-31).

* We may, like Jesus, be 'crucified', but no one can take our life away. What matters is that, like Jesus, we love.

The king will say to those at his right hand, 'Come, you that are blessed by my Father, inherit the kingdom prepared for you from the foundation of the world; for I was hungry and you gave me food, I was thirsty and you gave me something to drink, I was a stranger and you welcomed me, I was naked and you gave me clothing, I was sick and you took care of me, I was in prison and you visited me'. Then the righteous will answer him, 'LORD, when was it that we saw you hungry and gave you food, or thirsty and gave you something to drink? And when was it that we saw you a stranger and welcomed you, or naked and gave you clothing? And when was it that we saw you sick or in prison and visited you?' And the king will answer them, 'Truly I tell you, just as you did it to one of the least of these who are members of my family, you did it to me'. (Matthew 25:34-40)

* Jesus invites us to be with him, to walk with him. To do this we need to be enlightened, we need to see. 'They came to Jericho. As Jesus and his disciples and a large crowd were leaving Jericho, Bartimaeus son of Timaeus, a blind beggar, was sitting by the roadside. When he heard that it was Jesus of Nazareth, he began to shout out and say, "Jesus, Son of David, have mercy on me!" Many sternly ordered him to be quiet, but he cried out even more loudly, "Son of David, have mercy on me!" Jesus stood still and said, "Call him here". And they called the blind man, saying to him, "Take heart; get up, he is calling you". So throwing off his cloak, he sprang up and came to Jesus. Then Jesus said to him, "What do you want me to do for you?" The blind man said to him, "My teacher, let me see again". Jesus said to him,

"Go; your faith has made you well". Immediately he regained his sight and followed Jesus on the way' (Mark 10:46-52).

CHAPTER EIGHT

JESUS' CONCEPTION

The Letter to the Hebrews says of Jesus: 'He had to become like us his brothers and sisters in every respect' (Hebrews 4:15). What are we to make of the statements found in the Prologues of the Gospels of Luke and Matthew that speak of Jesus' conception by a virgin and God's Spirit? Are the Gospels asking us to believe that in this respect Jesus is not like us?

Luke writes: 'The angel Gabriel was sent by God to a town in Galilee called Nazareth, to a virgin betrothed to a man whose name was Joseph, of the house of David. The virgin's name was Mary' (Luke 1:26-27). She is told that she is to conceive one who 'will be called the Son of the Most High' (Luke 1:32). Mary says to the angel, 'How can this be, since I am a virgin?' The angel says to her, 'The Holy Spirit will come upon you, and the power of the Most High will overshadow you; therefore the child to be born will be holy; he will be called Son of God' (Luke 1:34-35).

In the *Apostles' Creed*, we declare: 'I believe in Jesus, God's only Son, who was conceived by the Holy Spirit, born of the Virgin Mary'. The faith of the Church is based on Luke's account. To be clear about our faith we need to ask: 'what is Luke asserting?'

The first point to make is that Luke is asserting that Jesus is the 'Son of God' – a teaching that recurs throughout Luke's Gospel and Acts; indeed, throughout the whole of the New Testament. In his account of Jesus' baptism, Luke states: 'A voice came from heaven: You are my Son, the Beloved; with you I am well pleased' (Luke 3:22). Likewise in his account of Jesus' transfiguration on Mount Tabor, the three disciples hear God declare: 'This is my Son, the Chosen; listen to him' (Luke 9:35). Jesus prays: 'All things have been handed over to me by my Father; and no one knows who the Son is except the Father, or who the Father is except the Son and anyone to whom the Son chooses to reveal him' (Luke 10:22). In a parable referring to himself as sent by God, Jesus states: 'The owner of the vineyard said, What shall I do? I will send my beloved son; surely they will respect him' (Luke 20:13). After describing Paul's enlightenment on the road to Damascus, Luke states 'immediately Saul began to proclaim Jesus in the synagogues, saying, 'He is the Son of God' (Acts 9:20).

We find the same teaching in Luke's teacher, Paul. A few examples should suffice. Paul writes: 'God revealed God's Son to me, so that I might proclaim him among the Gentiles' (Galatians 1:16). 'I live by the faith of the Son of God, loving me and giving himself for me' (Galatians 2:20). 'When the fullness of time had come, God sent his Son, born of a woman' (Galatians 4:4). 'God is faithful; by him you were called into the communion of God's Son, Jesus the Messiah, our LORD' (1 Corinthians 1:9). 'God has rescued us from the power of darkness and transferred us into the kingdom of his beloved Son' (Colossians 1:13). 'The Son of God, Jesus the Messiah, whom we proclaimed among you, was not "Yes and No"; in him it is always "Yes"' (2 Corinthians 1:19).

In the opening words of his Letter to the churches in Rome, Paul introduces himself: 'Paul, a servant of Jesus the Messiah, called to be an apostle, set apart for the gospel of God, which he promised beforehand through his prophets in the holy scriptures, the gospel concerning God's Son, who was descended from David according to the flesh and was declared to be Son of God with power according to the spirit of holiness by resurrection from the dead, Jesus the Messiah, our LORD' (Romans 1:1-4). Later in the same Letter we read: 'I serve God with my spirit by announcing the gospel of God's Son' (Romans 1:9). 'We were reconciled to God through the death of God's Son' (Romans 5:10).

So the first thing that Luke is asserting in the Prologue is that Jesus is the Son of God.

Luke's second point is that Jesus was conceived by the Holy Spirit. This is also at the heart of Christian faith. From his conception, Jesus is open to the intimate communion that God is offering him. It is to this intimate communion that we refer when we speak of the Holy Spirit.

Thirdly, Luke's account has something to say about Jesus' mother: she is a virgin. Does this mean that God miraculously intervened, bypassing Joseph, and enabling Mary to conceive Jesus while remaining physically a virgin? This is how Christians have traditionally understood it. Is that what Luke is asserting? It is important that faith seeks understanding. This must be a humble seeking for we are dealing with matters that concern God, and so are mysterious.

Our faith that Jesus is God's Son is not dependent on Mary's physical virginity. When we speak of God as Jesus' Father, we are asserting that everything that Jesus is, and everything he says and does comes from God. We are not speaking of biological paternity.

In the rest of the Prologue and throughout his Gospel and Acts, Luke does not refer again to Mary as a virgin. It is only stated here in Luke 1:26-35. Later in his Prologue, we are told: 'the child's father and mother were amazed' at what Simeon was saying about the child Jesus (Luke 2:13). We are told that 'every year Jesus' parents went to Jerusalem for the festival of the Passover' (Luke 2:41). Jesus went with them, but went missing. Luke writes that when 'his parents found him, his mother said to him: Child, why have you treated us like this? Look your father and I have been searching for you with great anxiety' (Luke 2:48). None of these texts leave us with the impression that Jesus' family life was unlike ours.

Another factor to consider is that Luke's Prologue introduces the reader to key theological assertions that are central to his presentation of Jesus in his Gospel. Its focus is not on biography. Luke's powerful stories prepare the reader for his interpretive commentary.

Furthermore, again and again the New Testament speaks of Jesus as 'the Son of God', but Mary's virginity is never mentioned by Mark, never mentioned in the Gospel of the Beloved Disciple, never mentioned by Paul in any of his letters. We find no mention of it in any of the other letters in the New Testament, or in the Apocalypse. Jesus being the Son of God is at the heart of the teaching of the New Testament. We cannot claim the same for Mary's virginity.

To understand Luke's purpose in presenting Mary as a virgin we need to examine the thinking of those for whom he is writing. Luke's readers were familiar with legends that stated that the founders of the great cities of the Greco-Roman world had a god for their father and a virgin for their mother. Romulus and Remus are celebrated as twin brothers, the sons of a vestal virgin named Rhea Silvia and the god Mars. Asclepius was the son of Apollo. His mother was the virgin Coronis. Helen was the daughter of Zeus and Leda. Alexander, the Ptolemies, and the Caesars were said to have been 'virgin-born'. Is Luke speaking of Mary as a virgin to state, using language that his readers would understand, that it is Jesus who is divine (the Son of God), not the heroes of their myths, or their emperors?

Virgil (70-19BC) writes that shepherds heralded Augustus's birth. His birth is called 'good news' ('evangelion'). Augustus the new-born child is proclaimed saviour (soter) and described as LORD (kyrios). He is seen as the bringer of a new age of peace. He is called the son of God. He shows exceptional qualities at the age of twelve, and so it goes on. In his *Lives of the Caesars*, Suetonius (69-122AD) says that there were prophecies and portents before the birth of Augustus, whose conception was miraculous. It took place in the context of worship at a temple. Upon his birth, Augustus was declared to be a King and a Ruler. Luke mentions Augustus (Luke 2:1) to tell his readers to look to Jesus, not Augustus, as their 'saviour' and 'peacemaker'.

There is one other place where Mary is called a virgin. It is in the Gospel of Matthew, but, once again, it is only in the Prologue, not in the body of the Gospel. Commenting on Matthew's prologue, Ulrich Luz writes: 'We do not need to assume that this story, which strongly follows traditional schemas, contains information from the circle of Jesus' family. Nor are the signs favourable for the historicity of the virgin birth ['virginal conception'], which in the New Testament is transmitted only by Matthew and Luke ... It is probably part of the attempt of Jewish Christian communities to bear witness to Jesus who was appointed by God as Son according to the Spirit (Romans 1:4) in a way that was analogous to other ancient stories in the form of an infancy narrative. The virgin birth [conception] then is a means of confessing faith and has no historical background' (*Commentary on Matthew*, Fortress Press 2007, volume I, page 93).

We have already quoted from the Letter to the Hebrews: 'Jesus had to become like his brothers and sisters in every respect' (Hebrews 2:17). 'We have a high priest who in every respect has been tested as we are, yet without sin' (Hebrews 4:15). This is picked up in the teaching of the Second Vatican Council: 'The Son of God worked with human hands, thought with a human mind, acted with a human will, and loved with a human heart. He has truly been made one of us, like to us in all things except sin' (The Church in the Modern World (*Gaudium et Spes*) n. 22 par 2).

In portraying Mary as a virgin in language familiar to his audience, Luke reinforces his focus on God as Jesus' 'Father', and on Jesus' intimacy with the one he called 'Abba'. Luke's scene of the virginal conception is also a beautiful way of portraying the special relationship between Mary and God. A virgin is a person who gives their first love to another. Mary's first love was for God, and the conception of Jesus was a fruit of that special love. Would that every conception came from such a communion!

François Bovon in his Commentary on Luke in the *Hermeneia Series* 2002 (volume 1, page 45) writes: 'Biblical marriages are sometimes spiritualised in the Hellenistic Judaism of Egypt, where sexual vocabulary is applied to the mystical union with God. In Philo it becomes clear that births like that of Isaac were regarded as virgin births; for Philo himself these are only an allegory of the ecstatic union of the soul with God'.

In repeating Luke's description of Mary as a virgin, is the Christian community (however it has imagined this over the centuries) been keeping before us the intimate relationship between Jesus and the God he called 'Abba'; a communion that we speak of when we refer to the Holy Spirit?

CHAPTER NINE

JESUS' MIRACLES

If we believe with the author of the Letter to the Hebrews that 'Jesus had to become like his brothers and sisters in every respect' (Hebrews 2:17), what are we to make of Jesus' miracles? Is he like us in this? In this respect, are we unlike him?

When we call something a 'miracle', we are saying two things: it arouses wonder, and we cannot explain it. The surprise of a miracle alerts us to something that is ever present but which our achieved knowledge can obscure: namely, that it is the initiative of God (the ultimately mysterious) to which we are responding in everything we do and seek to do. It is our longing for communion with God that is the mainspring of our desire to know and love.

If we think of God as an object, we think of God intervening, sometimes in response to our prayer, and demonstrating God's presence and action in the world by setting aside what we have come to speak of as the 'laws of nature'. There are two things wrong with this thinking. The first is that when we speak of the so-called 'laws of nature', we can forget that they are only models that we construct to describe what we experience. They do not claim to exhaust the dynamism of nature or the relationships, processes, and causal inter-connectedness of the natural world. The second is that God is not intervening from outside, but is constantly present and active in creation. It is up to us to be open to God's presence and action. When we are, wonderful things can happen. It is a matter of our being open to welcome God's action in our lives, not hoping and waiting for God to intervene. Jesus revealed God as Self-giving Love. Creation is an explosion of this Self-giving love.

Since God is Love, a person who is open to this love and welcomes it can provide for others a space in which they can experience love. If they welcome it, there is no limit to what divine love can bring about in their lives, a love that can heal mind and heart and body. We should not be surprised at the effect someone as pure and loving as Jesus can have on those who are open to welcome love. Furthermore, Jesus asked his disciples to love others with his love. There is no reason to think that the miracles that occurred when people encountered Jesus should set him apart from us. He is showing what can happen when anyone is open to welcome God's love into their life.

On one occasion when Jesus brought healing and peace to a person whose psyche was broken, the Pharisees accused him of acting with the power given him by the prince of demons. Jesus responded: 'If I cast out demons by Beelzebul, by whom do your own exorcists cast them out?' (Matthew 12:27). Obviously Jesus was not the only one who brought healing. In fact there are people with special powers of healing in every culture. What stands out in Jesus' case is that his healing flowed from the purity and power of his love.

We become what we are called to be to the extent that we love, to the extent that, like Jesus, we 'participate in the divine nature' (2 Peter 1:4). There is more to the matter than this, as we will see when we examine the miracles recounted in the Gospels, but this is the key consideration. Paul writes: 'Hope does not disappoint us, because God's love has been poured into our hearts through the Holy Spirit that has been given to us' (Romans 5:5). Miracles show what love can do when we welcome it.

We are called to share Jesus' communion with God, and, loving with his love, we are called to love others, thereby offering them the space where they can be open to God's life-giving, healing love. As Jesus said: 'The one who believes in me will also do the works that I do, and, in fact, will do greater works than these' (John 14:12). Paul writes: 'God supplies you with the Spirit and works miracles among you by your believing what you heard' (Galatians 3:5). Paul includes miracles among the manifestations of the Spirit given us for the common good (1 Corinthians 12:10). 'We have this treasure in clay jars, so that it may be made clear that this miraculous power belongs to God and does not come from us' (2 Corinthians 4:7). 'The LORD said to me: My grace is sufficient for you, for power is made perfect in weakness. So, I will boast all the more gladly of my weaknesses, so that the power of the Messiah may dwell in me' (2 Corinthians 12:9).

There is something else that we must note before we come to reflect on the Gospel accounts. In 1984, the Pontifical Biblical Commission wrote the following: 'The Gospel traditions were gathered and gradually committed to writing in the light of Easter, until at length they took a fixed form in four booklets. These booklets do not simply contain things "that Jesus began to do and teach" (Acts 1:1); they also present theological interpretations of such things. In these booklets, then, one must learn to look for the Christology of each evangelist ... Authors whose writings are preserved in the New Testament have interpreted the deeds and sayings of Jesus in diverse ways' (*Theological Interpretations in the Gospel Traditions: Scripture and Christology* 2.2.2.2.b).

The Gospels are a record of what Jesus said and did, but they are also texts that express the understanding of Jesus that the Gospel writers set out to convey to their readers. To do this, they frequently draw on imagery contained in the Hebrew scriptures. They do this to link what Jesus does with the rich traditions contained in the scriptures. They want to portray Jesus as the new Moses and the promised Messiah. They also use all the resources of rhetoric, poetry and drama available to them. The Gospels are not snapshots of Jesus' life. They are portraits that use language that expresses the faith and love of the Christian communities, for they want to attract their readers to embrace Jesus and share his communion with God.

Miracles of healing

Paul writes: 'God was in Jesus, his Messiah, reconciling the world to God' (2 Corinthians 5:19), initiating what Paul dares to call 'a new creation' (Romans 8:19), a new sinless way of expressing the yearning of creation for communion with God.

The Gospels are full of accounts of people being healed. So intimate is Jesus' communion with God and so beautiful is the love with which he embraces everyone, that people find their hearts open to want to welcome his love and so share his communion. The effect of this openness is that they experience healing in their mind, heart and body.

In his account of the beginning of Jesus' ministry, Matthew gives us the following summary statement: 'The people brought to Jesus all the sick, those who were afflicted with various diseases and pains, those possessed by demons, epileptics and those who were paralysed, and he cured them' (Matthew 4:24). Luke writes: 'They were all trying to touch Jesus, for power came out from him and healed them'

(Luke 6:19). 'God anointed Jesus of Nazareth with the Holy Spirit and with power; and he went about doing good and healing all who were oppressed by the devil, for God was with him' (Acts 10:38). At the first Pentecost, Peter speaks to the crowd about 'Jesus of Nazareth, a man attested to you by God with miracles, wonders, and signs that God did through him among you' (Acts 2:22).

There is no doubt that it is God, the source of our being, who is doing the healing. Such was Jesus' presence and love that people were encouraged to open their hearts to God dwelling in them and gracing them to 'live and live to the full' (John 10:10). Their 'faith' opened them to healing.

Miracles of healing do not set Jesus apart from us. On the contrary, Jesus wanted to share with his disciples the healing power he experienced, a power that he believed was flowing from his communion with God. He encouraged them to open themselves to the kind of intimacy he experienced and to share in his generous loving of others so that they, like him, would be able to attract the sick to believe in God's love for them and find healing. Matthew writes (10:1, 6-7): 'Jesus summoned the twelve disciples and gave them authority over unclean spirits, to cast them out, and to cure every disease and every illness.' Jesus sent them on mission: 'As you go proclaim the good news: The kingdom of heaven has come near. Cure the sick, raise the dead, cleanse the lepers, cast out demons'.

Jesus' contemporaries thought of sickness as being due to the influence of 'spirits' or 'demons'. This thinking was widespread in the first century Mediterranean world, and beyond. The word 'demon' was used especially in the case of people experiencing extreme irrational feelings or suffering from a sickness that affected their psyche. A demon is also referred to as an 'unclean spirit' (Mark 1:23), or 'the spirit of an unclean demon' (Luke 4:33). The Gospels speak of 'Beelzebul, the ruler of the demons' (Mark 3:22-23). The mindset is complicated by reference to devils. In the wilderness Jesus encounters 'Satan' (Mark 1:13). Matthew calls him 'the tempter' (Matthew 4:3) and the 'devil' (Matthew 4:5; see Acts 10:38)'. This is a complex area due to the many influences that came to Judah especially from Persia and Greece.

The power to heal extended beyond Jesus' immediate disciples. Luke writes: 'God did extraordinary miracles through Paul' (Acts 19:11). Paul reminds the Christians in Corinth: 'The signs of a true apostle were performed among you with utmost patience, signs and wonders and mighty works' (2 Corinthians 12:12). To the Christians in Rome he writes: 'I will not venture to speak of anything except what the Messiah has accomplished through me to win obedience from the Gentiles, by word and deed, by the power of signs and wonders, by the power of the Spirit of God' (Romans 15:18-19). Jesus is the vine. We are the branches. We are all invited to cling to the vine, and so to share Jesus' intimacy with God and Jesus' love. A fruit of this love is miraculous healing.

Peter speaks of 'Jesus of Nazareth, a man attested to you by God with miracles, wonders, and signs that God did through him among you, as you yourselves know'(Acts 2:22). The author of the Letter to the Hebrews states: 'God added his testimony by signs and wonders and various miracles, and by gifts of the Holy Spirit, distributed according to his will' (Hebrews 2:4). Let us watch Jesus.

* A psychically disturbed man finds healing (Mark 1:21-27; Luke 4:31-37). Jesus is in the synagogue in Capernaum. Also present is a man who is described as having 'an unclean spirit'. We

are told that they were astounded at Jesus' teaching. In a separate episode recorded in the Gospel of the Beloved Disciple, we read what happened when the Pharisees sent the temple police to arrest Jesus. The police return without Jesus and when they are challenged they say: 'never has anyone spoken like this' (John 7:46). We are not given the content of Jesus' words in the synagogue. No doubt it was what came to be called the 'good news'. Hearing Jesus speak so beautifully of God's love and seeing Jesus witnessing to this love by his manner, the disturbed man experiences a profound peace and healing. We should not be surprised at the healing that flows from what Jesus understood as his intimate communion with God.

* Peter's mother-in-law is healed from a fever (Mark 1:29-31; Matthew 8:14-15; Luke 4:38-39). Mark writes that Jesus 'took her by the hand and lifted her up'. Luke adds that 'Jesus rebuked the fever' (Luke 4:39), implying that her sickness was brought about by a 'spirit' or 'demon'. Jesus' presence and his touch is enough to cause her to recover from the fever and experience the joy of being able to offer hospitality to Jesus and his disciples. The episodes recorded in the Gospels are chosen for the light they throw on Jesus' ministry and how it affected people. In this scene, we find the word 'serve' (*diakonein*), a word used throughout the New Testament to refer to 'ministry'. There is more to healing than making people feel physically well. It is about living to the full, and this includes giving oneself to others in

love. Peter's mother-in-law is the first person in the Gospel who witnesses to this; the first 'deacon'.

* 'That evening, at sundown ... Jesus cured many who were sick with various diseases, and cast out many demons' (Mark 1:32, 34). Jesus' presence and the power of his love invites people to believe in God's desire to offer them healing of body and mind. Immediately after this scene the Gospels focus on Jesus' prayer (Mark 1:35-39; Luke 42-44). The gospel-writers do not want us to forget that everything Jesus was, everything he said, and everything he did, including healing, flowed from his communion with God and his commitment to follow the inspiration of God's Spirit.

* Mark concludes his first chapter with an account of Jesus' healing a man whose condition excluded him from association with people (Mark 1:40-45; Matthew 8:1-4; Luke 5:12-16). He had some form of virulent skin complaint. It caused fear, for the discolouration of the skin reminded people of death. There must have been something extraordinarily attractive about Jesus for this 'leper' to disobey what everyone took as God's law (see Leviticus 13), and to brave the outrage of the people by approaching Jesus. He must have been confident that Jesus would not reject him and that Jesus' touch would heal him and restore him to the community. We hear him say to Jesus: 'If you want to you can make me clean'. The manuscripts vary in describing Jesus' reaction. Some have him being profoundly moved with anger – presumably for the

way we human beings hold onto distorted images of God. Others have him profoundly moved with compassion. Jesus replies: 'Of course I want to. Be made clean'. Imagine the man's feelings when Jesus embraces him. Jesus' love and the man's welcome of this love (what the Gospels call 'faith') issues in healing. Jesus paid a price for his action, for he had to suffer being banished from the community for coming into contact with a 'leper' (see Leviticus 5:3). However, such was Jesus' attraction that the people disregarded the law 'and came to Jesus from every quarter' (Mark 1:45).

* A centurion's servant is healed (Matthew 8:5-13; Luke 7:1-10; compare John 4:46-53). A centurion approaches Jesus and tells him of his servant who is 'lying at home, paralysed, in terrible distress' (Matthew 8:6). Jesus was touched by the centurion's love for his servant, and was amazed at the man's 'faith'. He assures him that his servant will recover. Jesus' presence is healing, as is his touch. This scene reminds us that Jesus' word has its own healing power.

* The healing of a man 'paralysed' by sin (Mark 2:1-12; Matthew 9:1-8; Luke 5:17-26). Four men bring a paralysed man to Jesus. From Jesus' response we learn that this is not an ordinary paralysis: 'When Jesus saw their faith, he said to the paralysed man: Your sins are forgiven' (Mark 2:5). Miracles can happen only where there is faith. God is always present, holding us in existence and gracing us to live a full life in communion with God. We are

not praying that God will reveal God's presence by intervening. We are praying that we, and those we love, will be open to whatever love God is offering. Grace is always present. It is effective only when it is welcomed, and sometimes, for reasons that escape us, welcoming of love issues in healing.

Those who witnessed the healing of the paralysed man 'were all amazed and glorified God'. We are meant to look deeper than to the man's physical state. Jesus could see people's longing for a deeper freedom that could come only through communion with God. It was Jesus' faith, Jesus' love that encouraged them to believe. The man was healed from sin; that is to say, from whatever it was that was hindering the fullness of life that Jesus knew and to which we are all called. When people are open to God, God's love flows to them through Jesus. It is God, the One who is the source of our existence, who offers everyone fullness of life, which, as in this scene, includes healing from whatever is a barrier to love.

In a later scene when Jesus comes to Nazareth, we are told: 'Jesus could do no miracle there, except that he laid his hands on a few sick people and cured them. He was amazed at their unbelief' (Mark 6:5). Essential to a miracle is that a person accepts to be drawn into communion with God. When Jesus' authority is challenged, he tells the paralysed man to 'stand up, take your mat and go to your home' (Mark 2:11). As we watch this scene, we are moved to pray that we be freed from the paralysis of sin and enabled to take the next step of love.

* The healing of a man with a withered hand (Mark 3:1-6; Matthew 12:9-14; Luke 6:6-11). Once

again we are in a synagogue and it is the Sabbath day. There is a man in the synagogue with a withered hand. It was assumed that this was a punishment from God because of some sin. As always, Jesus is attracted to anyone who is oppressed. Those with hearts that are closed to Jesus are watching him to see whether he will cure the man on the Sabbath, so that they might accuse him. Jesus risks everything for love and the man is healed. As in every scene in the Gospels, this scene is included because of its symbolic value. We can have a 'withered hand', just as we can be 'paralysed by sin'. A 'withered hand' impedes action. We cannot do what we know we should do, or what we really want to do. We are assured by this Gospel that Jesus is holding our hand, holding us in God's love. We may not be able to do what we want to do, or what others expect of us, but, like Jesus on the cross, we can always do what God graces us to do, and in the final analysis that is all that matters.

* A man is healed at the pool of Beth-zatha (John 5:1-9). The man is described as having been ill for thirty-eight years. This was the time the Israelites wandered in the wilderness after leaving the oasis of Kadesh-barnea till they reached Moab (see Deuteronomy 2:14). He symbolises all of us on our journey to the 'Promised Land'. Jesus asks the man (as he asks us): 'Do you want to be made well?' The man explains why he has remained sick so long and Jesus tells him: 'Stand up, take your mat and walk.' He has been in the wilderness far too long. Jesus

wants him, as he wants us, to enter the Promised Land: to enjoy the inheritance God wants for us, to 'live to the full' (John 10:10).

* A blind man is healed after washing in the pool of Siloam (John 9:7). In this scene, as often in the Gospels, blindness symbolises a need to be enlightened. Enlightenment comes with baptism, symbolised in this story by the water in the pool of Siloam, where he is told to bathe.

* Jesus brings peace to the tortured mind of a man in the Gentile country east of the lake (Mark 5:1-20; Matthew 8:28-34; Luke 8:26-39). The scene that precedes this portrays Jesus rebuking the wind and calming the sea (see Mark 4:35-41; Matthew 8:23-27; Luke 8:22-25). That scene assures us that, whatever the chaos might be that surrounds us, it cannot take us from God's love. We will look at that scene later.

This scene in the Gentile country focuses on the inner chaos that disturbs our mind and heart. Does this take us from God's love? The man is described as being possessed by a legion of 'unclean spirits'. He is afraid of the power he sees in Jesus, but he knows he wants it, and at the end of the scene we see him sitting with Jesus 'clothed and in his right mind' (Mark 5:15). Internal chaos cannot separate us from the love of God. We need Jesus' love to heal us by enabling us to welcome God's love, which is always present. Whatever our situation, we have to stop asking the wrong question: "Why is God allowing this?" Who said God is allowing it? God has given us freedom and people can abuse their freedom by acting against God's will. The real question is: "Where is God in this situation?" and the answer is: "Where there is love, there is God". Whatever our situation, let us look for love, for that is where we will find God. This deranged man found love in Jesus.

* Not even death can separate us from God's love (Mark 5:21-43; Matthew 9:18-26; Luke 8:40-56). Two events from Jesus' ministry are linked. The first concerns a woman who is experiencing a flow of blood from her body, which is meant to be a vehicle of life, not death. She dares to touch Jesus' garment and Jesus says to her: 'Your faith has made you well; go in peace and be healed of your disease' (Mark 5:34). The second concerns a young girl who is declared dead. In the presence of his disciples and the girl's parents (Mark 5:37, 40), Jesus takes the girl by the hand and says 'Talitha, cum (Little girl, arise)' (Mark 5:41). Mark is determined to distance Jesus from the charlatans who claimed to heal by using magic formulas. Jesus speaks in Aramaic, his own native tongue and that of the girl.

This scene is demonstrating what Paul declares: 'I am convinced that death cannot separate us from the love of God in the Messiah Jesus our LORD' (Romans 8:38-39). It is not meant to raise our hopes that, when the time comes for us to die, we will be brought back to this life. The Gospel writers are encouraging their communities to trust that the risen Jesus will be there on the other side of death, and that he will take us by the hand and raise us to share his risen life ('arise!'). Paul declares: 'Jesus must reign until he has put all his enemies under his feet. The last enemy to be destroyed is death' (1 Corinthians 15:25-26). 'Death has been swallowed up in victory. 'Where, O death, is your victory? Where, O death, is your sting?' (1 Corinthians 15:54-55). Jesus believed that the source of our life is God. We can destroy our life if we obstinately refuse to welcome God's Presence and action in our lives. But nothing we do can stop God loving us. Like the little girl, let us take Jesus' hand as he reaches out to us, and let him share with us his life.

* Jesus' healing ministry (Mark 6:54-56; Matthew 14:35-36). 'People recognised Jesus, and rushed about that whole region and began to bring the sick on mats to wherever they heard he was. And wherever he went, into villages or cities or farms, they laid the sick in the marketplaces, and begged him that they might touch even the fringe of his cloak; and all who touched it were healed.'

* Two blind men are able to see (Matthew 9:27-31). When we compare this with Matthew's account of the two men who were possessed by demons (see Matthew 8:28), and the two blind men later in the Gospel (Matthew 20:13), it is interesting to speculate that Matthew is writing for communities such as that in Antioch that are composed of Jewish and Gentile Christians. Is one of the men representing the Jews and the other the Gentiles? As Matthew presents these scenes, is he making the point that communities can be blind as well as individuals?

* Jesus fulfils in his person what was expected of the Messiah (Matthew 11:5; Luke 7:22). In his response to a question posed by John the Baptist Jesus says: 'Go and tell John what you hear and see: the

blind receive their sight, the lame walk, the lepers are cleansed, the deaf hear, the dead are raised'. Matthew has carefully laid the ground for Jesus' reply. We have seen the blind receiving their sight (9:27-31). We have seen the lame walking (9:2-8). We have seen a leper cleansed (8:2-4), the deaf hearing (9:32-34), and the dead being raised (9:18-26).

We have also heard Jesus send his disciples out to do what we have witnessed Jesus doing. Jesus wants us to be like him in this, and so he shares with us his communion with God: 'Cure the sick, raise the dead, cleanse the lepers, cast out demons' (10:8). Miracles happen because Jesus' presence and love inspire people to get in touch with the longings of their hearts, and so with God. Far from separating Jesus from us, miracles witness to what can happen in anyone's life. We are all graced to share in Jesus' prayer and love, and when we do there is no limit to what prayer and love can make possible.

* The daughter of a Syro-Phoenician woman is healed (Mark 7:24-30; Matthew 15:21-28). Typical of the thinking of the time, her daughter is said to be sick because she has an 'unclean spirit', a 'demon'. In Matthew's account, Jesus hesitates to respond to her request because his understanding of God's will is that his mission was 'only to the lost sheep of the house of Israel' (Matthew 15:24). He does not act except in response to God's will as it is revealed to him. This is what happens here. Jesus is surprised by her faith and is inspired to say to her: 'Woman, great is your faith; let it be done for you as you

wish' (Matthew 15:28). Jesus was always open to the surprise of God's gift.

* A deaf and dumb man is healed (Mark 7:32-35; Matthew 15:29-31). As in the scene with the twelve-year-old girl, the Gospel writers are keen to demonstrate that Jesus is not a magician, a master of spells. Jesus addresses the man in ordinary everyday Aramaic: 'Ephphatha (Be opened)! (Mark 7:34). 'The crowd were astounded beyond measure, saying, 'He has done everything well; he even makes the deaf to hear and the mute to speak' (Mark 7:37).

* A young man is brought to Jesus, suffering, it seems, from epilepsy (Mark 9:14-29; Matthew 17:14-20; Luke 9:37-43). His father speaks of him having a 'spirit that makes him unable to speak' (Mark 9:17). Jesus' presence and love bring healing to the boy: 'Jesus took him by the hand and lifted him up, and he was able to stand' (Mark 9:27). Here, as in every scene we have watched, our focus is on Jesus' communion with God and his compassionate love. The disciples were unable to help the boy. Jesus explains that there is a direct connection between healing and prayer (Mark 9:29). Jesus' loving presence encouraged the father to open his heart to God present in him and in his son. A miracle of healing flowed from this communion.

* Sight is restored to a blind man outside Jericho (Mark 10:46-52; Matthew 20:29-34; Luke 18:35-43). The man cannot heal himself and he knows it. He cries out for mercy. He is taken to Jesus who, with profound respect, asks him: 'What do you want

me to do for you?' (Mark 10:51). As we reflect on this scene, we get in touch with our own need for enlightenment. We saw once, but, like the man in this scene, we need to 'see again'. Something in the tone of Jesus' voice, something in Jesus' presence draws this man into communion with him, and so with God. 'He regained his sight and followed Jesus on the way' (Mark 10:52).

Conclusion

The Letter to the Hebrews says of Jesus: 'He had to become like us his brothers and sisters in every respect' (Hebrews 4:15). In the previous chapter, we looked at what Luke and Matthew were affirming when they spoke of Jesus' mother as a virgin. We questioned the common understanding that Jesus' conception was unlike ours. In this chapter, we have argued that the miracles of healing that God worked through Jesus do not separate Jesus from us. God wills miracles of healing to happen through all of us, and that this would happen God draws us into intimate communion with Jesus, God's Son. At the Last Supper, Jesus is quoted as saying: 'Very truly, I tell you, the one who believes in me will also do the works that I do and, in fact, will do greater works than these' (John 14:12). We have seen what wonderful things happened when people encountered Jesus. We have also seen that they happened because of what flowed out of Jesus' communion with God. Jesus wants everyone to experience this divine communion, and he calls his disciples to so love people that they will get in touch with God and with God's love for them, and find and give healing.

Dramatic portraits expressing the Gospel-writers' insight into the person of Jesus

If the following scenes are read as factual eye-witness accounts of episodes that took place in Jesus' life and ministry, we would have to question the author of the Letter to the Hebrews when he writes that Jesus 'had to become like his brothers and sisters in every respect' (Hebrews 2:17). He goes on to say that Jesus can sympathise with our weaknesses because he has been 'tested in every way that we are, yet without sin' (Hebrews 4:15). We would also have to question the statement from the Council of Chalcedon (451 AD) that Jesus' divinity did not alter his humanity. As we have noted a number of times, far from altering his humanity, it was Jesus' divinity (his intimate communion with his Father) which is at the core of his humanity, and it is Jesus' mission to draw us into his divinity so that we can share his Spirit and live, like him, a life of self-giving love, 'in the image of God'.

It is important to look again at the statement, quoted earlier, from the Pontifical Biblical Commission: 'These booklets do not simply contain things "that Jesus began to do and teach" (Acts 1:1); they also present theological interpretations of such things'. In the portraits on which we are about to meditate, the gospel-writers are portraying fundamental aspects of who Jesus is, what he reveals about God, and what it means to be a disciple.

The gospel-writers belong to a story-telling culture. Think of the marvellous stories found in the Book of Exodus. This is something that Jesus was quite at home with, as we see from his use of parables. I am not sure that 'parable' is a good word to describe the following scenes, but they are powerful symbolic stories. The question we are invited to ask is not 'What exactly happened?' but 'Why is the gospel-writer portraying the scene in this way? What is he saying about God, about Jesus, and about us?'

* Jesus is an icon of God the bridegroom, pouring his love into our thirsty hearts (John 2:1-11). The Beloved Disciple begins his account of Jesus' ministry by presenting two contrasting scenes. The second scene, in which we see Jesus clearing the temple, is found in the other Gospels at the end of Jesus' public ministry. The Beloved Disciple places it at the beginning, so that he can present a stark contrast with his opening scene – a wedding feast. The central point of the good news goes beyond the Torah, beyond finding our security in a religious system symbolised by the temple. The Beloved Disciple wants us to see God as a Bridegroom. God is Love, and it is Jesus who knows this– in the biblical sense of 'know': he is conscious of being profoundly loved, and he believes that the source of this love is God, the Bridegroom, the Lover of Israel. The ancient covenant, represented by the six water jars, has fulfilled its purpose. We need something more than water. We are thirsty for the 'wine' of the Spirit, and Jesus is ready to begin his ministry ('has not my time now come?'). His ministry is to attract people to open their hearts to the gift of life that God is offering them. Jesus knows this divine love and he wants everyone to know it.

* Jesus rebukes the wind and calms the sea (Mark 4:35-41; Matthew 8:23-27; Luke 8:22-25). 'On that day, when evening had come, Jesus said to his disciple:

"Let us go across to the other side". Leaving the crowd behind, they took him with them in the boat, just as he was. Other boats were with him. A great windstorm arose, and the waves beat into the boat, so that the boat was already being swamped. Jesus was in the stern, asleep on the cushion. They woke him up and said to him: "Teacher, do you not care that we are perishing?" Jesus woke up and rebuked the wind, and said to the sea: "Peace! Be still!" Then the wind ceased, and there was a dead calm. He said to them: "Why are you afraid? Have you still no faith?" They were filled with great awe and said to one another: "Who then is this, that even the wind and the sea obey him?"'

When Mark composed this dramatic scene, the Jewish-Roman war was being waged in Palestine, and Christians in Rome were suffering persecution. Mark is not writing to raise hopes that the persecution will stop. He is calling on his readers not to lose faith in the God who is embracing them when they embrace Jesus. Jesus' prayer in his agony did not stop his being crucified, but it did keep him open to God's love, which was expressed in raising him from the dead. Paul was convinced that 'nothing can separate us from the love of God in the Messiah Jesus' (Romans 8:39). The gospel-writers are assuring us that we need not give way to instinctual fear. Faith inspires us to look beyond our weakness and turn to Jesus, for the risen ('awakened') Jesus is with us. No storm, no external chaos, can separate us from God's love. God is present to us as we face the storms of life. We have to face them, but we must not forget to call on God whose love is present whatever our situation.

It is clear from the primeval narrative of creation (Genesis1:2,6-8) and that of the flood (Genesis 6-9), that the sea was for the Jews a symbol of chaos, and therefore of the evil which tries to resist God's creative and redeeming action. In the scene before us, Jesus is with us as we venture out into the midst of chaos. He is also taking his disciples to the 'other side' - the Gentile side, the country thought of as 'unclean', at the mercy of evil spirits. The waves are portrayed as hurling themselves against the boat, seeking to destroy Jesus and his disciples. Jesus is clearly unafraid. The same cannot be said of his disciples. Jesus may appear not to hear our cry, but the awakened (risen) Christ is truly caring: the forces of evil cannot take God's love from us.

Many elements of the story are borrowed from dramatic images found in the Hebrew scriptures. We are watching the Creator vanquishing the sea monster. Addressing God, the psalmist says: 'You rule the raging of the sea; when its waves rise, you still them. You crushed Rahab like a carcass; you scattered your enemies with your mighty arm' (Psalm 89:9-10). Jesus 'rebukes' the wind - an expression we find in Psalm 104:7 where the word of the Creator God rebukes the waters of chaos and they flee before his command. God also rebukes the waters of the Red Sea (Psalm 106:9).

Again and again in the Gospels, we hear Jesus repeating a phrase often found in the Hebrew scriptures: 'Do not be afraid!' (see Mark 5:36; 6:50). It is fear that enslaves us. We may be powerless to prevent the storms that overwhelm us, much as Jesus was powerless to avoid crucifixion. We are not powerless, however, in the way we respond. In this scene, we are encouraged to cry out to the One who alone can save us. Whatever might be happening around us and to us, Jesus is with us in the boat. He does care for us. He wants to save us.

An appropriate reflection on this scene can be found in the prayer of Jonah, whose lack of faith provoked a storm similar to the one in our Gospel narrative: 'I called to the LORD out of my distress, and ... you heard my voice. You cast me into the deep, into the heart of the seas, and the flood surrounded me; all your waves and your billows passed over me. Then I said, "I am driven away from your sight ... The waters closed in over me; the deep surrounded me ... As my life was ebbing away, I remembered the LORD; and my prayer came to you ... Deliverance belongs to the LORD!"' (Jonah 2:2-9; see also Psalm 107:23-30).

The miracles we have reflected on show the healing power of God offered through Jesus' love to anyone who believes. The storm on the lake encourages us, whatever our situation, to keep believing in the presence of Jesus in our lives. Jesus offers us his trust, his faith, his love, his communion with God. Nothing can take this from us.

* Jesus feeds the multitude (Mark 6:33 to 7:37; Matthew 14:13-21; Luke 9:10-17; John 6:5-13). Like the scene of the storm, this scene, too, is packed with allusions to the Hebrew Bible, especially the narrative of God feeding the people in the wilderness by sending them the manna (Exodus 16). There are allusions as well to the Christian celebration of the Eucharist. It is a dramatic portrayal of God's longing to nourish us by the gift of his Son, the 'bread' we really need, as we, like the Israelites, journey to the Promised Land.

There must be hundreds of memories lying behind this powerful scene: memories of the many times that Jesus nourished people by his smile, his compassion, his words and his deeds. All his close followers had stories to tell of the miraculous way in which he touched their hearts, fed their deepest hunger and quenched their deepest thirst. And there was no limit to his generosity in providing for them, as there was no limit to the love that he showed to them. He believed that he drew on the Spirit of God in his own ministry, and he shared this Spirit with others 'without measure' (John 3:34).

By the time the Gospel was written, Jesus' disciples could also call on their own memories of how Jesus' Spirit, living in them, had worked similar miracles in their lives. This is the point made in the account which concludes with the Twelve having a basket each, full of bread to continue feeding the hungry people (Mark 6:42). Jesus' disciples had found that they too had been God's instruments in miraculous ways, in nurturing people as they journeyed towards God through the desert of this world. Nothing is impossible to God. Our talents, our hands, our hearts, our love, our acts of service can bring sustenance to a hungry world. It is radically important that we know that we do not, of ourselves, have the resources to do this. It is equally important to know that we are not left to ourselves. Jesus, who was with his disciples, is with us. United to him and caught up in his prayer, we too can praise and thank God; we too can mediate Jesus' love to each other.

* Jesus walks on the sea (Mark 6:45-52; Matthew 14:22-34; John 6:16-21). 'Jesus made his disciples get into the boat and go on ahead to the other side, to Bethsaida, while he dismissed the crowd. After saying farewell to them, he went up on the mountain to pray. When evening came, the boat was out on the sea, and he was alone on the land. When he

saw that they were straining at the oars against an adverse wind, he came towards them early in the morning, walking on the sea. He intended to pass them by. But when they saw him walking on the sea, they thought it was a ghost and cried out; for they all saw him and were terrified. But immediately he spoke to them and said: "Take heart, it is I; do not be afraid". Then he got into the boat with them and the wind ceased. And they were utterly astounded, for they did not understand about the loaves. Their hearts were hardened.'

In the Exodus tradition, there is a close connection between the giving of the manna and the crossing of the sea. The slaves escape from Egypt across the Red Sea (Exodus 14:15-31) and then are fed by God in the wilderness (Exodus 16). Here the scenes are reversed. It is the nourishment from heaven that makes possible the journey to freedom.

The disciples are in the boat (symbol of the church). Jesus appears not to be with them. He is the resurrected Jesus 'on the mountain' enjoying communion with God. Even though Jesus is no longer with us in the way he was before his death, the gospel-writers use this dramatic story to demonstrate that he is still caring for the community. We will be safe if we do not lose faith in him. This scene focuses on Jesus' divinity: his intimate sharing in God's life. This is clear from the words he uses: 'It is I; do not be afraid'. 'It is I' translates the Greek *ego eimi* (I AM), which is linked in the Greek version of the Old Testament to the Hebrew divine name, YHWH (see Exodus 3:11-15 and Isaiah 43:8-13).

In Jesus, we see God walking upon the waters of chaos (Psalm 77:19; Job 9:8; 38:16; Sirach 24:5-6). By the power of

God, Jesus is able to master the chaos. The disciples, gripped by fear, anxiety and near-despair, have to learn that they, too, can 'walk on water', they, too, can reach the Promised Land, provided they put their faith in him and not in themselves. How often they would have experienced this while Jesus was living with them and after his death. Jesus remained in prayer, and so, trusting in God, he was able to rise above the persecution and suffering that he endured; he was able to 'walk on the sea'. With him, they could do the same.

This vivid portrayal of the struggling community and the divine Jesus coming to its rescue reminds us of the following passages, taken from the Isaiah scroll: 'Thus says the LORD, he who created you, O Jacob, he who formed you, O Israel: Do not fear, for I have redeemed you; I have called you by name, you are mine. When you pass through the waters, I will be with you' (Isaiah 43:1-2). 'Awake, awake, put on strength, O arm of the LORD! Awake, as in days of old, the generations of long ago! ... Was it not you who dried up the sea, the waters of the great deep; who made the depths of the sea a way for the redeemed to cross over? So the ransomed of the LORD shall return, and come to Zion with singing; everlasting joy shall be upon their heads ... The oppressed shall speedily be released; they shall not die and go down to the Pit, nor shall they lack bread. For I am the LORD your God, who stirs up the sea so that its waves roar – the LORD of hosts is his name' (Isaiah 51:9-10, 14-15).

Jesus comes to them only in the last hours of darkness, just before dawn. The impression one has is that he brings the light with him, as well as enabling them to reach the shore, but only after they have spent the night battling the seas in the dark. There is a divine wisdom in the timing of grace, and it seems that we all must go through a dark night to make us realise that we are totally incapable of reaching our destination on our own, and we are quite incapable, on our own, of letting go and admitting our powerlessness. There seems to be no other way to learn this lesson, except to be made to face the darkness alone. If we are willing to dare this journey in the night, God will not release us from it till our entire being cries out for that release and recognises that God alone can bring it.

As in previous scenes, the purpose of this portrait is to strengthen our faith in Jesus, and so in God. Matthew adds the following scene: 'Peter said: "LORD, if it is you, command me to come to you on the water". Jesus said: "Come". So Peter got out of the boat, started walking on the water, and came toward Jesus. But when he noticed the strong wind, he became frightened, and beginning to sink, he cried out: "LORD, save me!" Jesus immediately reached out his hand and caught him, saying to him: "You of little faith, why did you doubt?"' (Matthew 14:28-31). Like Jesus we can 'walk on water', provided we keep our eyes fixed on Jesus.

* Death cannot separate us from God's love, and so from life (John 11:1-44). In the last of the dramatic and symbolic presentations of Jesus' ministry given us by the Beloved Disciple, Jesus' friend Lazarus dies and is buried. This is not the end of Lazarus' life, for physical death cannot separate us from God, the source of our life. We hear Jesus declare: 'I am the resurrection and the life. Those who believe in me, even though they die, will live' (John 11:25). Jesus summons Lazarus: 'Lazarus, come out!' (John 11:43). As with the anecdote of the twelve-year-old girl, so here, we are not being encouraged to hope that we will be restored to this life. Rather, we are being invited to open our hearts to welcome Jesus,

knowing that, if we share his life, nothing can separate us from God, the source of our life.

CHAPTER TEN

JESUS DIED AS HE LIVED

Jesus' final meal with his disciples

From the beginning of Jesus' ministry, the religious leaders had been looking for an opportunity to have him arrested and killed (see Mark 3:6). Matters came to a head when pilgrims were gathering in Jerusalem to celebrate Passover. Jesus and his followers were among them. Jesus caused a stir in the temple court when 'he entered the temple and began to drive out those who were selling and those who were buying in the temple, and he overturned the tables of the money changers and the seats of those who sold doves; and he would not allow anyone to carry anything through the temple' (Mark 11:15-16). Jesus demanded that the temple should not be used for commercial transactions, but should be a 'house of prayer', and 'for all the nations' (Mark 11:17). For the religious leaders this was the last straw. They dared not run the risk of a disturbance on the Passover, which that year coincided with the Sabbath, so they resolved to capture Jesus and have the Roman authority crucify him before the festival. They were successful, for they persuaded the Roman governor that Jesus was a dangerous rebel, and Jesus was crucified on the Friday about noon (John 19:14), just as the lambs for the Passover were being killed.

The Beloved Disciple's account of the Last Supper

A letter written from within the community of the Beloved Disciple opens with the following words: 'We declare to you what was from the beginning, what we have heard, what we have seen with our eyes, what we have looked at and touched with our hands, concerning the word of life. This life was revealed, and we have seen it and testify to it, and declare to you the eternal life that was with the Father and was revealed to us. We declare to you what we have seen and heard so that you also may have fellowship with us; and truly our fellowship is with the Father and with his Son Jesus Christ. We are writing these things so that our joy may be complete' (1 John 1:1-4).

The Beloved Disciple's account of the Last Supper is a good example of something that he is sharing with us so that our 'joy may be complete'. The Beloved Disciple was reclining next to Jesus at the Supper, so close that he could lean back against Jesus' breast and converse intimately with him (John 13:23-26). As we reflect on chapters 13 to 17 of his Gospel, we are invited to be the Beloved Disciple, for in Jesus' eyes that is what we are. Let us accept this invitation and take our place next to Jesus to celebrate with him his final meal.

The Beloved Disciple begins his account of the meal with the words: 'Jesus had always loved those who were his in the world, but now he showed how perfect his love was' (John 13:1). On Mount Sinai, the people under the leadership of Moses undertook to enter into a covenant with God. God would be their God and they would be God's people. God pledged love to them, and they pledged themselves to welcome that love and to respond in love. Jesus' final meal is to celebrate a new and more intimate covenant. Our commitment is also more intimate. It is to love one another the way Jesus loves us, or, rather, it is to allow the love he gives us to transform our hearts so that we will love others with his respect, intimacy and gentleness. Jesus is showing his love for us right through to the end. He pleads with us to do the same for others, for his heart reaches out to the world and he knows that if he is to carry out his Father's mission, he will have to continue it through us.

The Beloved Disciple begins by focusing on the loving way Jesus washed his disciples' feet, an act that typified his affection for them. In laying aside his outer garments and taking them up again, Jesus is making a symbolic gesture, for he wants us to know that he is willing to lay aside his life for us and take it up again so that he can continue to pour the Spirit of his love into our hearts as we carry on his life and his mission: 'I give you a new commandment, that you love one another. Just as I have loved you, you also should love one another. By this everyone will know that you are my disciples, if you have love for one another' (John 13:34-35). The love he wants us to experience is the love he shares with God: 'I am in the Father and the Father is in me' (John 14:11). He assures us that God will give us a share in the Spirit that binds him to God: 'The Spirit abides with you; the Spirit will be in you' (John 14:17). 'You will know that I am in my Father, and you are in me, and I am in you' (John 14:20). 'My Father will love you, and we will come to you and make our home with you' (John 14:23).

Reflecting on the Last Supper and preparing his readers for Jesus' crucifixion and death, the Beloved Disciple has Jesus say to his disciples (and so to us): 'Do not let your hearts be troubled. Believe in God. Believe also in me' (John 14:1). We can share in Jesus' communion with God, for we experience Jesus' own Spirit in our hearts, the Spirit who is the love binding Jesus and his Abba. Jesus promises to pray in us. Experiencing his prayer, we will experience his intimate communion with God (John 14:16-23). John records Jesus reminding his disciples that he is the vine and we are the branches. If we cling to him, we will bear the fruit of love (see John 15:5). 'As the Father has loved me, so I have loved you; abide in my love' (John 15:9).

Jesus knew that his disciples were not yet strong enough to continue believing in God after his death: 'The hour is coming, indeed it has come, when you will be scattered, each one to his home, and you will leave me alone' (John 16:32). To sustain them, he went on immediately to remind them of his intimate communion with God: 'Yet I am not alone because the Father is with me'. It was this love that would enable him to go through the crucifixion, and it would be the same love that would sustain them.

The whole of John 17 is a prayer expressing Jesus' longing for us to enjoy his communion with God. However deep our longing it cannot compare with the longing of Jesus' heart that 'the love with which you, Father, have loved me may be in them, and I in them' (John 17:26). Jesus thanks God for his mission to give eternal life 'to all you have given me' (John 17:2). 'Father, the words that you gave to me I have given to them and they have received them and know in truth that I came from you; and they have believed that you sent me' (John 17:8). Jesus wanted only one thing: to share with people what he had come to know about God. His beautiful humanity was such that he drew people to him, but only so that he could get them in touch with God who was gracing them to 'live to the full' (John 10:20). He wanted people to know that he was on a mission from God. He wanted to share with everyone his divinity: 'As you, Father, are in me and I am in you, may they also be in us' (John 17:21). 'You have loved them even as you have loved me' (John 17:23).

Jesus prays to his Father: 'that the love with which you have loved me may be in them, and I in them' (John 17:26).

The Synoptic account of the Last Supper

Because the meal was on the occasion of the festival of Passover, the Synoptic Gospels portray it as a Passover meal. There was no lamb, because the lambs were not available till the afternoon of the following day. There was no need for a lamb, since Jesus was there: 'the Lamb of God who takes away the sin of the world' (John 1:29).

Jesus wants to reassure the disciples that his death does not mean that he would not continue to be present among them, nurturing them with his love. He knows that they will always need his presence and the comfort and strength of his Spirit to motivate them to keep on loving. So, when he breaks the bread this night, he offers it to them, to us, promising that whenever we come together to break bread in this way, he would be with us, nourishing us with his love, with his prayer and with his Spirit. He gives himself to us: he gives us his body. To eat this bread is to open our hearts and minds and bodies to receive him into the very centre of our lives where he will continue to nourish us and to transform us by this intimate communion.

He then offers us the cup of blood-red wine. His heart will be pierced, torn apart not just by the soldier's lance but by the callous indifference of so many to the truth, and by our rejection not only of Jesus but of God's love which filled Jesus' heart. He offers the cup to us his disciples so that when we drink in the future from this cup it is his lifeblood which we will be drinking, his life poured out for us, his Spirit which he is offering us to nourish our love.

Jesus' Agony in Gethsemane

We repeat here Mark's account of Jesus' agony in Gethsemane: 'They went to a place called Gethsemane; and Jesus said to his disciples: Sit here while I pray. He took with him Peter and James and John, and began to be distressed and agitated. And said to them: I am deeply grieved, even to death; remain here, and keep awake. And going a little farther, he threw himself on the ground and prayed that, if it were possible, the hour might pass from him. He said: Abba, Father, for you all things are possible; remove this cup from me; yet, let your will not mine be done' (Mark 14:32-36).

Clearly Jesus does not want to die. He said once: 'I came to bring fire to the earth, and how I wish it were already kindled!' (Luke 12:49). He had been faithful to love, but to what effect? The religious leaders stubbornly resisted his message. The crowd was as fickle as ever. There was no apparent change in the Roman occupation and the resistance to it. Jesus' disciples weren't ready to carry on his mission. Whatever grief Jesus was experiencing and whatever was agitating him, he came, through his prayer, to a place of peace: 'let your will not mine be done'. He determined to carry out his mission, to do his Father's will, come what may! Whatever the religious and civil powers would do; Jesus knew what he would do. He would continue to carry out the mission given to him by God. He would continue to embrace sinners. He would continue to reveal God as a God of love. He would continue to challenge those who stubbornly resisted God's love for themselves and for others. He would continue to believe in the God whose love he experienced at his baptism and throughout his ministry.

What is God's will? Is Jesus saying that he doesn't want to die, but, since his Father wants him to die, he will obey?

Peter does not support this distorted understanding: 'God has glorified his servant Jesus, whom *you* handed over and rejected in the presence of Pilate, though he had decided to release him. But *you* rejected the Holy and Righteous One and asked to have a murderer given to you, and *you* killed the Author of life, whom God raised from the dead. To this we are witnesses' (Acts 3:13-15). God's role is seen in the resurrection. Jesus' death was brought about by the Jewish leaders, the Roman prefect and the fickle crowd!

Stephen's message is the same: 'You stiff-necked people, you are forever opposing the Holy Spirit, just as your ancestors used to do. Which of the prophets did your ancestors not persecute? They killed those who foretold the coming of the Righteous One, and now you have become his betrayers and murderers' (Acts 7:51-52).

Likewise Paul: 'You became imitators of the churches of God in Christ Jesus that are in Judea, for you suffered the same things from your own compatriots as they did from the Jews, who killed both the LORD Jesus and the prophets, and drove us out; they displease God' (1 Thessalonians 2:14-15).

Listen to Jesus' parable: 'The owner of the vineyard sent slaves to collect the produce ... Some they beat, others they killed. He had still one other, a beloved son. Finally, he sent him to them, saying: Surely, they will respect my son. But those tenants said to one another: This is the heir; come, let us kill him, and the inheritance will be ours. So they seized him, killed him, and threw him out of the vineyard' (Mark 12:6-8).

The mission given to Jesus was to reveal God's love, not to die on a cross. Jesus confronts his enemies: 'You are looking for an opportunity to kill me'. This is not because it is part of God's plan. On the contrary, it is 'because there is no place in you for my word' (John 8:37). Crucifying Jesus was a terrible injustice, and, as the psalmist knows: 'You are not a God who delights in sin' (Psalm 5:4).

Earlier in the book, we emphasised Jesus' obedience. He emerged from the agony determined to continue to carry out his Father's will. The author of the Letter to the Hebrews writes: 'In the days of his flesh, Jesus offered up prayers and supplications, with loud cries and tears, to the one who was able to save him from death, and he was heard because of his reverent submission. Although he was a Son, he learned obedience through what he suffered' (Hebrews 5:7-9).

In the agony, he struggled. Perhaps he felt he had failed to carry out the mission given him by God. Did he wonder whether he should have refrained from emptying the temple? Was he too hard on the priests? We are not invited into the details of his struggle. What we do know is that he emerged from the agony resolved to continue the mission given him by God. His Father's will has nothing to do with a crucifixion. That was a terrible miscarriage of justice, and so, by definition, against God's will. God's will is that Jesus continues to reveal God as love. He rose from his prayer resolved to keep eating with sinners, to keep hugging lepers, to keep on loving people out of their despair and the sin that so easily paralyses, to keep challenging those who try to confine God within the limits of their traditions. He was determined to do this, come what may! The tragedy is that the Jewish Council refused to listen, the Roman governor was too weak to reject the demands of the Jewish leaders, and the crowd was too frightened not to follow the instructions of their leaders. But all this was offset by the amazing love that Jesus displayed throughout the so-called 'trials' and on the cross.

Jesus' dying on the cross

Let us meditate now on the meaning of Jesus' dying. We are asking who he is: his final moments are a perfect statement of the answer. There, on the cross, we see his love, we see his communion with God, we see his faith and trust and obedience in perfect clarity. His manner of dying is his last word, his final statement about what it is to be a man; and his final revelation of God.

The Beloved Disciple's account of Jesus' dying

Before reading this section, it would be good to read slowly through the account of Jesus' passion and death as recorded in John chapters 18 and 19. Then, while keeping before our eyes the image of Jesus on the cross, we might go back and meditate on chapters 13 to 17. These chapters are intended by the Beloved Disciple to be reflections on the meaning of the cross, and it is helpful to imagine some of these words as being spoken by Jesus while he is offering up his life.

If we look only superficially at what is happening on the hill of Calvary, we might turn away with despair in our eyes. For the cross is a symbol of all that is ugly in the human condition. We see the abuse of religious and civil power, and the pride and petty pretensions of people who are frightened of the truth. We see an innocent man being murdered. All the pain of a broken, hurt, frustrated, lost world breaks over us. Questions about the meaning of life become acute. Does the life of the man dying there have any meaning? What was the good of all his words, and his love, and his dreams? And what value is there in the lives of those responsible for his death? When we look at Jesus on the cross, we can be forgiven for wondering if there is any hope for anyone. All our most cherished hopes are called into question.

Yet the Beloved Disciple saw something else. His eyes were fixed on the figure around whom everything was happening, and his main impression was of love: 'The hour had come for Jesus to pass from this world to the Father. He had always loved those who were his in the world, but now he showed how perfect his love was' (John 13:1).

In spite of the ugliness, the violence, and the stupidity of it all, this scene is about love; and the Beloved Disciple knows it. Jesus has given of himself, day in and day out. Now he is hanging there, a free man, innocent of evil amid injustice. Whatever others were doing to him and about him, he kept believing: believing in people, believing in the world, believing in himself. He kept believing in God, and the Beloved Disciple could hear Jesus still praying to this God as 'Abba'. He had given everything; now he was giving his life. The two thieves were there to remind everyone that Jesus belongs to his world; he belongs to us. But belonging to us, he shows finally and conclusively that sin is not the inevitable consequence of being human that we all thought it was. From the cross, Jesus shows anyone who cares to stand there and contemplate him, that you don't have to despair. Physical death cannot take away life. Life is a gift from God the life-giver.

Jesus was rooted in love and built on love, and he remained in love on the cross. That is what the Beloved Disciple remembered. In the reality of the pain, suffering, failure, rejection, accusations, injustice, and all the apparently meaningless absurdity of the crucifixion, Jesus was in peace. He felt for those who were lost in it all, he spoke words of forgiveness and reconciliation; he kept striving to piece together the broken fragments of people's lives, right to the end.

The Beloved Disciple was desolate. The one who had given meaning to his life was being violently taken from him. But there was something about the way Jesus looked at him that said: 'Do not let your heart be troubled. Trust in God still, and trust in me' (John 14:1). 'Peace I bequeath to you, my own peace I give you, a peace the world cannot give, this is my gift to you. Do not let your heart be troubled or afraid' (John 14:27). 'You are sad now, but I shall see you again, and your heart will be full of joy, and that joy no one shall take from you' (John 16:22). 'Be brave: I have conquered the world' (John 16:33)

The Beloved Disciple as he stood at the foot of the cross realised something he had heard often enough, but that had never before really penetrated his heart: I am worth dying for! The world is worth loving and loving unto death! God was being revealed there on Calvary. Here were our ultimate questions being answered. His heart was breaking, and so was that of Jesus. But what he saw there and heard there remained in his memory as the ultimate revelation of God, the ultimate experience of meaning.

The Beloved Disciple had scattered with the rest, in fear. But then he met Jesus' mother, and her need as well as his need for her made him brave the crowd. Together they walked with Jesus through the city gate and out to the quarry and graveyard where Jesus was to die. He would never forget Jesus' final gift: 'Seeing his mother and the disciple he loved standing near her, Jesus said to his mother: Woman, this is your son. Then to the disciple he said: This is your mother' (John 19:26). A simple gesture, a love-gift from the heart, a sacred trust. And in it was the answer to his deepest quest. The one who had given him so much love needed him, wanted him, expected of him.

The Beloved Disciple's life must have meaning. Jesus gave it meaning: 'And from that moment the disciple made a place for her in his home' (John 19:27). It was as though John had no choice now but to do what Jesus had often told him to do: 'Love just as I have loved you' (John 13:34 and 15:12).

Then Jesus died. How the Beloved Disciple loved him then! Jesus had said once: 'If you love me you will be loved by my Father, and I will love you and show myself to you' (John 14:21). Now, as he stood there, holding and being held by Jesus' mother, something happened that burst upon him and lifted him up. Seeing Jesus, he saw the Father revealed.

'One of the soldiers pierced Jesus' side with a lance; and immediately there came out blood and water' (John 19:34). Zechariah the prophet had dreamed of the ultimate gift of peace that God would pour out on his people. He described the darkness and the battle of evil against good. Even God's anointed would be killed. But God's word would stand forever: 'I will pour out a spirit of kindness and prayer. They will look on the one whom they have pierced; they will mourn for him as for an only son, and weep for him as people weep for a firstborn child. When that day comes there will be great mourning. When that day comes, a fountain will be opened up for sin' (Zechariah 12:10-11, 13:1).

The heart of Jesus is the heart of God. When all that people could do to pierce the heart of God had been done, from the living heart of the glorified Jesus, his life-blood and the spring of living water poured out over the Beloved Disciple and Mary and over the world, to cleanse, to nurture, and to give life. This was the Spirit that Jesus had promised: 'If anyone is thirsty, come to me! Come and drink, you who believe in me! As scripture says 'From his breast will flow fountains of living water' (John 7:37-38). From the disciple's breast, yes. But only because it first comes from the breast of Jesus.

Jesus had said: 'I live and you will live' (John 14:19). The Beloved Disciple knew it that day. The one whom his heart had loved was alive, in the embrace of God, in the bosom of his Father. From the cross Jesus drew the Beloved Disciple into that same embrace. And from that hill, he had no choice but to go out to everyone and draw them into the same mystery. He had seen God. He knew that 'God is love' and that eternal life, life without limit, was given to him from the cross, and was offered to anyone who believed. 'We saw his glory, the glory that is his as the only Son of the Father, full of grace and truth. No one has ever seen God; it is the only Son, who is in the bosom of the Father, who has made God known' (John 1:14, 18).

Truth (Greek: *aletheia*) is revealed when what is real is not forgotten because it is not hidden behind deceptive appearances. Glory (Greek: *doxa*) is a manifestation of truth that is so radiant and so beautiful that it arouses wonder and praise. Jesus had revealed the truth about God from the time that his disciples first met him (John 2:11), but never more radiantly, never more convincingly, and never more gloriously, than in the way he gave his life from the cross. This was Jesus' hour of glory (John 11:4, 13:31-32, 17:1), for his dying revealed the extent and quality of his relationship with his Father, and it revealed the truth about the God in whom Jesus placed his trust. In the words of the author of the Letter to the Hebrews, Jesus, giving his love and his life from the cross, is 'the radiant light of God's glory' (Hebrews 1:3). There we see 'the glory of Christ, who is the image of God. God's glory, the glory on the face of Christ' (2 Corinthians 4:4, 6).

To say that Jesus on the cross is revealed as the only begotten Son of God, is to say that he is revealed there as the living, and life-giving image of his Father. Jesus did not spare his life, and so we come to know God as one who does not spare God's own life but pours it out for us even to giving us his own Beloved Son, taking the risk that we might hurt him, but giving him to us to love us all the same. As Paul says: 'God did not spare God's own Son but gave him up to benefit us all' (Romans 8:32).

Paul speaks for the Beloved Disciple, and for everyone who looks upon the crucified Jesus, when he writes: 'Now I can live for God. I have been crucified with Christ, and I live now not with my own life but with the life of Christ who lives in me. The life I now live in this body I live by the faith of the Son of God, loving me and sacrificing himself for my sake. I cannot bring myself to give up God's gift' (Galatians 2:19-21).

The Synoptics' account of Jesus' dying

In the Synoptics, there is no mention of Jesus' mother or the Beloved Disciple being by the cross. Luke does say that 'his friends stood at a distance' (Luke 23:49). Some women are mentioned as being there, mourning his death, but the overall impression is of Jesus dying utterly alone and forsaken.

Mark and Matthew refer their readers to Psalm 22, the cry of the poor man. The reader may wish to pray through the psalm (see pages 93-94), listening to the words as coming from the heart of Jesus on the cross. It captures the agony and the ecstasy, the abandonment and the joyful recognition of God's abiding presence.

The Synoptics all speak of the tearing of the temple veil. As we contemplate Jesus on the cross, the veil stopping us from seeing God is torn. We can now see God revealed and revealed as unconditional Love. The only thing that can stop us experiencing the intimacy of communion with God that Jesus experiences is our stubborn refusal to open our hearts to the love that never stops being offered to us. The veil that hid the face of God has now been removed. Gazing on the face of Jesus giving his life on the cross, anyone who wants can now see the face of God and live. Who God is has now been revealed for all to see.

They also observe that it is the Roman centurion, the non-believer, who recognises the presence of God in Jesus. There is hope for us all!

Jesus is remembered as being faithful to the end. He kept believing in God; he continued to care for people; he kept trusting and praying and hoping and loving. He showed us that not even death can separate us from the love of God, and in doing so he gave us the final and convincing proof of the truth of all that he had ever said or done.

It was not Jesus' death that revealed God, it was 'the way he died' (Mark 15:39). It was the way he gave his life that powerfully symbolised the way he had given his life day in and day out to redeem people from 'sin' and draw them into the saving embrace of God, an embrace into which he yielded his own life from the cross.

May we be able to pray with Paul: 'It is no longer I who live. It is Christ who lives in me. And the life I now live in the flesh I live by the faith of the Son of God, loving me and giving himself for me' (Galatians 2:20).

Conclusion

To attempt to answer the question 'Who is Jesus', we must begin with his prayer, his communion with God, the Spirit of love that he shared with his Father, his divinity. His disciples came to see that the source of Jesus' life, his words and actions, was his fidelity to the mystical experiences that he believed flowed from his communion with God. He saw that if we are to be free from whatever is holding us back from living a full and productive life we must stay in touch with our heart and believe that we are loved. This is key to all the Gospel portraits of Jesus, and he was faithful to his mission till he could say from the cross: 'It is accomplished' (John 19:30).

Note

If Jesus' life ended with his death on the cross, we would be asking 'Who *was* Jesus?' However, as the following chapter will demonstrate, Jesus' disciples had experiences after Jesus' death that convinced them that Jesus was, mysteriously but truly, alive and active in their lives. For the past two thousand years, people have had similar experiences. So, as we explore the way Jesus' disciples portrayed him in the New Testament, we are asking 'Who *is* Jesus?' Let us turn now to the accounts of these post-crucifixion experiences found in the New Testament.

CHAPTER ELEVEN

JESUS THE CRUCIFIED ONE WHO LIVES

The Gospels contain very little on the period following Jesus' death. Each gospel-writer has a section on the empty tomb describing how the women came to the tomb on the first day of the week following the Sabbath only to find that the body of Jesus was not there. The meaning that the empty tomb came to have for Jesus' disciples is portrayed in a vision in which it is revealed to the women that Jesus whom they are seeking is alive, still held in existence by God and enjoying communion with God. This tells us what the early church believed. If we wish to know why, we have to move on to the texts that portray the ways in which the disciples experienced Jesus as still present and active in their lives.

Mark ends his Gospel (16:8) with the empty tomb and the promise that the disciples will see Jesus in Galilee. A conclusion (Mark 16:9-20) was added later, which, while having its own perspective, is derived from the other Gospels.

Matthew has only one short scene portraying an encounter with Jesus on a mountain in Galilee (Matthew 28:16-20). Jesus commissions the Eleven to go to the whole world with the gospel – the good news – promising to be with them. We are told that when they 'saw him, they fell down before him, though some hesitated' (Matthew 28:17). It might appear that Matthew is describing the kind of encounter we are used to, with the normal sense experiences of seeing and hearing, though with a mysterious air about the whole scene. But is that doing justice to the portrait? We note the significance of mountains in Matthew's Gospel: the mountain of temptation (Matthew 4:8), the mountain from which the new Law was proclaimed (Matthew 5:1), the mountain on which it is declared that Jesus fulfils the Law and the Prophets (Matthew 17:1-8), and the mountain of prayer whence came Jesus' saving action (Matthew 14:23). Does Matthew mention the 'hesitation' to indicate that the kind of 'seeing' he is speaking about is a faith-illumination, an awareness of Jesus' presence and of his empowering them to carry on his mission? What is the nature of the experience portrayed by Matthew?

Luke gives us two scenes. The first presents us with two despondent disciples journeying from Jerusalem to Emmaus. Someone joins them, walks with them, lifts up their hearts by explaining the scriptures to them and helping them to understand the significance of the crucifixion, and finally shares a meal with them. At the meal, they recognise that the person is Jesus. They hurry back to tell the community and are assured that it was indeed Jesus because 'The LORD has risen and appeared to Simon' (Luke 24:34). There are quite mysterious elements in the portrait. We are told that their eyes were prevented from recognising him while he walked with them (Luke 24:15-16) but were 'opened' at the evening meal. They realised who it was 'but he had vanished from their sight' (Luke 24:31).The symbolism in the portrait is obvious enough, especially the journey, the Eucharist, and the authority of the assembly. But how are we to understand the experience itself? Can we conclude that the risen body of Jesus has the same basic qualities as the body we now know, such that Jesus can walk, has much the same physique, and can converse, and eat; but that his voice and face are somehow different?

In Luke's second portrait, Jesus is present with the assembled community. As in Matthew, there is some hesitation, and doubts were arising in their hearts (Luke 24:38). Jesus reassures them that it really is himself and shows them the wounds that he bore for them. To prove that he is not a ghost, but is truly alive, he invites them to touch him and he eats with them. Are we to conclude from this that our hands can actually touch the body of a person who is in the life beyond death? Are we to conclude that the Risen Jesus has the capacity to eat and digest the kind of food we eat? Is Luke stating that as a fact, or is that the imagery he uses to assert that what they experienced was indeed someone who is alive, and not a ghost from the underworld? In his conversation with them, Jesus 'opened their minds to understand the scriptures' (Luke 24:45). He spoke of the gift of the Spirit and the power of forgiveness, and he commissioned them to carry on his mission. Finally, he withdrew from them and was taken up into heaven. Once again, the symbolism is clear. Our question centres on the nature of the experiences portrayed in this richly symbolic literature.

The Gospel of the Beloved Disciple also has two scenes. The first is a personal encounter between Jesus and Mary of Magdala. We are told that 'she saw Jesus standing there, though she did not recognise him' (John 20:14). In fact, she comes to recognise him only when he calls her by name. The second scene is very like that of Luke. Jesus appears to the assembled community, speaks of peace, the gift of the Holy Spirit and forgiveness, and shares his mission with them. The element of doubt finds expression in a separate encounter which focuses on Thomas who learns to believe when he is invited to put his finger into the wounds that Jesus bears in his hands and put his hand into Jesus' pierced side. Is the text describing an actual physical encounter? Does the risen body of Jesus have qualities like those we now associate with our body such that it can be touched? Or must we look deeper to grasp the meaning of these portraits?

Similarly with the scene in John chapter 21, an appendix to the Gospel. The disciples go back fishing. Jesus appears on the shore and instructs them how to catch fish. They are successful. Jesus is recognised by the Beloved Disciple. Peter swims ashore and there is an intimate encounter of reconciliation in which Jesus makes Peter the chief pastor of the flock. At the same time, we find this rather strange statement: "None of the disciples was bold enough to ask: Who are you? They knew quite well it was the LORD' (John 21:12). What is being asserting by this remark?

It is important to know how to read this literature in such a way as to enjoy the rich meanings that the portraits convey.

I: *The post-crucifixion experiences of Jesus' disciples*

Jesus' disciples did not follow him all the way to the cross. They lost heart, abandoned him and scattered. Yet, shortly after his death, we find them together again in Jerusalem. We find them speaking openly and enthusiastically about Jesus, telling everyone that he is alive. In speaking like this they encountered the same opposition that had engineered Jesus' death, but they would not be silenced. They stated clearly their conviction that the crucified Jesus has entered into life-beyond-death, the ultimate life with God. Furthermore, their preaching was convincing. History witnesses to the rapid and extraordinary growth and spread of Christianity. What happened to the disciples between their scattering and their coming together again? What did they experience that made such a powerful impression on them, gave them such courage and conviction, and carried them through persecution and even martyrdom?

The earliest account we have is in Paul's First Letter to the Corinthians: 'In the first place I taught you what I had been taught myself, namely that Christ died for our sins, in accordance with the scriptures; that he was buried; and that he was raised to life on the third day, in accordance with the scriptures; that he appeared first to Cephas and secondly to the Twelve. Next he appeared to more than five hundred of the brothers and sisters at the same time, most of whom are still alive, though some have died; then he appeared to James, and then to all the apostles; and last of all he appeared to me, too' (1 Corinthians 15:3-8).

Paul is listing those whose authority can be called on to guarantee the truth of his preaching concerning Jesus' resurrection. Cephas, the acknowledged leader of the Christian community, had come to see that Jesus was alive. So had the Twelve. The whole of the Jerusalem church had experienced Jesus' presence in their midst. So had James, the leading presbyter in the early Jerusalem community, and the many apostles who set out from Jerusalem to take the good news into the Jewish communities in Judea, Samaria and beyond. Finally, Paul himself, the apostle to the Gentiles (non-Jews), asserts that Jesus had manifested himself to him as well.

Jesus appeared first to Cephas

'Cephas' is the Hebrew word for 'rock' (in Greek *'petros'* whence 'Peter'). According to the Gospels, Peter was the first disciple to acknowledge his faith in Jesus. On that occasion, Jesus is portrayed as speaking of him as the rock on which the Church will be built (Matthew 16:17-19). The importance of Peter in the early community is apparent from the New Testament. Mark mentions him twenty-one times. The first half of the Acts concentrates on Peter's mission. In addition to the two letters that claim Peter as their author, we find him mentioned in Paul's Letter to the Galatians (1:18, 2:7-14) and also in his First Letter to the Corinthians (1:12, 3:22, 9:5). In the resurrection material, he has central place among the disciples. In Mark, the women at the tomb are told 'You must go and tell his disciples and Peter that he is going before you to Galilee' (Mark 16:7). In Luke, Peter's experience is presented as an assurance that what the Emmaus disciples assert is indeed true (Luke 24:34). We find an account of this experience in John chapter 21. The two features that this account highlights are Peter's experience of being forgiven, and his experience of being commissioned by the risen Jesus to carry out the task of leadership in the community.

All the Gospels record Peter's denial of Jesus (Mark 14:66-72; Matthew 26:69-75; Luke 22:55-62; John 18:15-18, 25-27). John chapter 21 tells us that Peter, having fled Jerusalem and gone back to Galilee, returned to his former occupation as a fisherman. It is as though he was trying to forget all about Jesus and the hopes and dreams they had shared. However, in a mysterious scene by the lakeside Jesus made his presence known to Peter. They shared a meal and after the meal 'Jesus said to Simon Peter: "Simon son of John, do you love me more than these others do?" Peter answered: "LORD, you know I love you". Jesus said to him: "Feed my lambs". A second time he said to him: "Simon son of John, do you love me?" He replied: "LORD, you know I love you". Jesus said to him: "Look after my sheep". Then he said to him a third time: "Simon son of John, do you love me?" Peter was upset that he asked him a third time: "Do you love me?" and said: "LORD, you know everything; you know I love you". Jesus said to him: "Feed my sheep" (John 21:15-17).

In his account of the Last Supper, Luke has Jesus say: 'Simon! Simon! Satan you must know has got his wish to sift you all like wheat; but I have prayed for you, Simon, that your faith may not fail, and once you have recovered, you in your turn must strengthen your brothers' (Luke 22:31-32). Peter's faith did not fail. He recovered and spent the rest of his life strengthening his brothers. Why? Because after Jesus' death, Peter experienced Jesus present in his life, forgiving him and entrusting him with his mission. We cannot, of course, hope to comprehend the many intimate and mysterious ways in which Peter was aware of the presence of Jesus, but it is these two aspects (being forgiven and being entrusted to carry out Jesus' mission) that are highlighted in the accounts we have. This experience of being loved, this enlightenment, led Peter to a faith-conviction that Jesus was alive. It also brought with it the power to transform his life and sustain him in his journey of discipleship.

Jesus appeared secondly to the Twelve

What happened to Peter seems to have happened to the others. The themes of forgiveness and mission recur in the post-crucifixion narratives. Luke speaks of the disciples being commissioned by Jesus to preach 'in his name, repentance for the forgiveness of sins to all the nations' (Luke 24:47). The Beloved Disciple writes: The disciples were filled with joy when they saw the LORD, and he said to them: 'Peace be with you. As the Father sent me, so I am sending you'. After saying this he breathed on them and said: 'Receive the Holy Spirit. For those whose sins you forgive they are forgiven'. Jesus insists on us forgiving. So much so that he adds: 'those whose sins you retain, they are retained' (John 20:23). We all know that if someone refuses to forgive us, a part of us feels bound. It is hard to be free. Jesus knows that his Father loves to forgive. He shows this in his ministry, and he wants his disciples to be like God in forgiving. We find the same theme in Peter's speeches in the Acts: 'It was the God of our ancestors who raised up Jesus to be leader and saviour, to give repentance and forgiveness of sins through him to Israel. We are witnesses to all this' (Acts 5:30-31; see 10:43).

It is a fact that after Jesus' death his disciples did continue his mission, and they understood it as a mission to free people from sin, from everything that trapped and distracted them and led them along a path that was futile and meaningless. The link between their despair at Jesus' death and their powerful and convincing witness was their own experience of being forgiven and commissioned by him.

The personal, intimate and religious nature of the experience of encounter with the risen Jesus is brought out in the stories that feature Mary Magdalene (John 20:11-18) and the Emmaus disciples (Luke24:13-35). The constant mention of doubt, hesitation, and non-recognition in the resurrection narratives highlights the need for a faith-illumination, a spiritual enlightenment, if a person is to recognise Jesus as present and active in their life.

Perhaps the most powerful and moving account of the conversion from doubt to faith is found in the final scene of the Gospel of the Beloved Disciple. It is the story of Thomas, told, no doubt, because it was typical of the conversion-journey experienced by many in those early days after Jesus' death. The other disciples had already encountered the risen Jesus. Thomas wants to see for himself: 'Unless I see the holes that the nails made in his hands, and can put my finger into the holes they made, and unless I can put my hand into his side, I refuse to believe' (John 20:25). Thomas wants to be convinced that it is Jesus of Nazareth, the crucified one, who is the one present to the disciples, forgiving them, calling them, commissioning them. Jesus manifests himself to Thomas and allows him the intimacy he requests. The scales fall from his eyes and in a profound religious experience he recognises the presence of God in the Risen Jesus: 'My LORD and my God' (John 20:28). He knew, with the knowledge of one who 'be-lieves,' that Jesus is indeed alive in the embrace of God. This Good News changed Thomas, brought him into the community and started him on his missionary activity.

Jesus appeared to more than five hundred

After Peter and the Twelve, the next authoritative witness to the resurrection is the whole community of those who knew Jesus before his death and experienced his risen presence. Luke gives us one description of their experience in the second chapter of the Acts. There he describes how they were filled with the Spirit of the risen Jesus on the feast of Pentecost, and how they began to preach in Jesus' name with courage and conviction. Jews gathered for the feast, and, while speaking different languages, they found a common understanding in conversion to Jesus and entry into the community of his disciples.

Another statement of the way in which the community experienced the risen Jesus is found in the conclusion to Mark's Gospel: 'the LORD Jesus was taken up into heaven: there at the right hand of God he took his place, while they, going out, preached everywhere; the LORD working with them and confirming their word by the signs that accompanied it' (Mark 16:19-20).

James, all the missionaries, and Paul himself

By the time Paul was writing his letter to the Corinthians, there had been over twenty years of missionary activity and thousands of people had experienced in their lives the presence and power of the risen Jesus. Paul reminds his readers of this and appeals to it as his final guarantee for the truth of his teaching (see 1 Corinthians 15).

Throughout the New Testament, the presence and influence of the risen Jesus is spoken of in terms of the Spirit of God. The Spirit (breath) is God as life-giver. The Spirit that was present in the community, giving it life, was Jesus' Spirit, the Spirit of love that unites him to his Father. The community of Jesus' disciples found themselves living Jesus' life, sharing his mission, experiencing his prayer and his power.

The Beloved Disciple concludes Jesus' prayer at the Last Supper with the words 'so that the love with which you, Father, loved me may be in them, and so that I may be in them' (John 17:26). That Jesus' prayer was answered can be seen from the following statement by Paul: 'Your interests are in the spiritual, since the Spirit of God has made a home in you. In fact, unless you possessed the Spirit of the Messiah you would not belong to him' (Romans 8:9; see Luke 12:12 and 21:14; Acts 16:6-7). The Spirit that gave life to the community was the Spirit of the risen Jesus. This is the 'power from on high' promised by Jesus (Luke 24:49). This is the Spirit that came down upon them at Pentecost (Acts 2). This is the Spirit that they could receive only after Jesus was glorified (John 7:38-39). The disciples found themselves becoming more and more like Jesus in their prayer, in their understanding, in their love; they found themselves healing as he had healed, liberating as he had liberated. The way they express it is to say that they were being transformed into him.

Paul writes: 'This LORD is the Spirit, and where the Spirit of the LORD is, there is freedom. And we, with our unveiled faces reflecting like mirrors the brightness of the LORD, all grow brighter and brighter as we are turned into the image that we reflect; this is the work of the LORD who is Spirit' (2 Corinthians 3:17-18). Paul speaks of the disciples as those chosen by God to be 'true images of his Son' (Romans 8:29). He speaks of them as 'God's work of art created in Christ Jesus to live the good life' (Ephesians 2:10). They are those who 'have the mind of Christ' (1 Corinthians 2:16). Paul says of himself: 'Life to me, of course, is Christ' (Philippians 1:21) and 'I have been crucified with Christ, and I live now not with my own life but with the life of Christ who lives in me' (Galatians 2:19). This, for Paul, was the essential characteristic of a disciple. He wrote to the Corinthians: 'Examine yourselves to make sure you are in the faith; test yourselves: Do you acknowledge that Jesus Christ is really in you? If not, you have failed the test' (2 Corinthians 13:5).

The love that characterised the Christian community was recognised as love from God, and as the love that characterised Jesus (Romans 5:5). The prayer that arose in their hearts was the prayer of Jesus (Romans 8:14-27), the prayer that caused them, like Jesus, to cry to God as 'Abba' (Romans 8:14-15; Galatians 4:6). They experienced a conversion in their lives: 'Now you have been washed clean, and sanctified, and justified through the name of the LORD Jesus Christ and through the Spirit of our God' (1 Corinthians 6:11). 'Remember it is God himself who assures us all and you, of our standing in Christ, and has anointed us, marking us with his seal and giving us the pledge, the Spirit that we carry in our hearts' (2 Corinthians 1:21-22). Paul prays: 'May the God of hope bring you such joy and peace in your faith that the power of the Holy Spirit will remove all bounds to hope' (Romans 15:13).

Behind all these references to the Spirit of God (the communion which the risen Jesus enjoys with God) lie the many ways in which Jesus' disciples experienced him as being alive in their midst and gifting them with his life. So it is that Matthew has the risen Jesus commissioning his disciples to go forth to the whole world baptising them, as Jesus himself had been baptised, with the overwhelming experience that God is indeed their Father. This is baptism in the Holy Spirit (Matthew 28:19). So it is that Luke has the risen Jesus promise: 'Now I am sending down to you what the Father has promised. Stay in the city until you are clothed with the power from on high' (Luke 24:49). So it is that John has Jesus breathe on the disciples and say, 'Receive the Holy Spirit' (John 20:22).

The Christian community is called the 'body of Christ'. In New Testament terminology the 'body' is that which is given life by the 'spirit'. We tend to think of our 'body' as confined within the physical limits of our flesh. Their idea was different. For them the 'body' means the self and includes everything that belongs to a person, everything that has its being from the 'spirit' of a person. When the Church is spoken of as a 'body', the reference is not to an organised corporation (though of course organisation is needed), but to the fact that the life experienced in the community is life given by the Spirit of Jesus. The Church is therefore the body of the Risen Jesus, in which the effects of his Spirit are realised. Every activity shared in by the Church has the effect of 'building up the body of Christ' (Ephesians 4:12; see also Romans 12:4-5, 1 Corinthians 10:16-17, 12:12-27, Ephesians 1:23, 2:16, 3:6, 4:4, 4:16, 5:23; Colossians 1:18, 1:24, 2:17, 2:19, 3:15).

In a special way, Jesus' disciples experienced themselves being the 'body' of Jesus when they gathered in his name and broke bread. It was in the assembly that they remembered Jesus as he had requested (1 Corinthians 11:25, Luke 22:19). It was there that the sacred scriptures were proclaimed, understood now in the light of Jesus' life, death and exaltation; it was there that their hearts burned within them as the meaning of Jesus' life and death and of their own was revealed to them. It was when they broke bread together that they shared his Spirit, each in their own way, for they knew that Jesus 'distributes different gifts to different people just as he chooses' (1 Corinthians 12:11). It was there that they experienced communion. It was there, especially, that they experienced his 'real presence' among them, nurturing them, inspiring them, forgiving them, and calling them into the intimacy of prayer. And it was from the assembly that they experienced the living Jesus sending them on a mission of love to spread the good news. As Paul writes: 'If we live by the truth and in love, we shall grow in all ways into Christ, who is the head by whom the whole body is fitted and joined together, every joint adding its own strength, for each separate part to work according to its function. So, the body grows until it has built itself up, in love' (Ephesians 4:15-16).

The gospel-writers capture this in their post-crucifixion accounts. It is 'while he was with them at table' in Emmaus that Jesus revealed his presence to the two disciples (Luke 24:30, 35). In the same way 'he showed himself to the Eleven themselves while they were at table' (Mark 16:14; see Luke 24:33; Acts I:4; John 20:19).

By the time Paul was writing his letters, and by the time the experiences of the communities had been reflected on, and told and re-told in the stories that found their way into the Gospels (the last third of the first century), many thousands of people had heard the good news as preaching spread throughout the Empire. Many thousands had been received into the community through baptism, experiencing reconciliation and forgiveness of sins and a conversion of life. Many thousands witnessed to the faith-inspired conviction and assurance that in all this it is Jesus himself who is at work. Their experiences were real. Their interpretation of them rested on the understanding of the first generation of followers who have 'been with us the whole time that the LORD Jesus was travelling round with us right from the time when John was baptising until the day when he was taken up from us' (Acts 1:21-22). It was these who recognised that the one forgiving, calling, inspiring and sending them was indeed Jesus of Nazareth.

Did Peter and the others in the immediate post-crucifixion period have quite distinctive experiences that were unlike anything Jesus' disciples have had since? No doubt this is possible. But it seems to me sufficient to say that Peter is the rock on which the Church is built (Matthew 16:18), and the apostles are the foundation of the Church (Ephesians 2:20), not because their post-crucifixion experiences of Jesus were different, but rather because it was they, and they alone, who could interpret those experiences. They were in a position to remember Jesus, to recognise his presence and action, and to link the one who was forgiving and inspiring them with Jesus of Nazareth. It is their faith-conviction, based on real, actual post-crucifixion experiences, that enables others since to recognise in their own experiences the presence of the living Jesus.

II: Ways of understanding and expressing post-crucifixion experiences

The Gospel portraits of the risen Jesus make it clear that those who experienced him were not dealing with a resuscitated Jesus, living again the kind of life he lived before his death and with the same kind of body. It is also clear from all the accounts that they were not experiencing a ghost, but rather a real, living, person. Some of the ways in which they express this truth could make us think that the risen body was very like the body we now experience. We must be careful not to let our imagination take over. We must also remember that we are looking at portraits, and not flipping through a photo album. Paul warns us: 'Someone may ask: How are dead people raised and what sort of a body do they have when they come back?' He adds: 'They are stupid questions' (1 Corinthians 15:35). The disciples insist that they experienced a real, living, person (in scriptural terms a living body); they are not claiming to describe the nature of the risen body, or explore the scientific question of the nature of matter.

With this caution in mind, let us explore four models used by the gospel-writers to speak of Jesus in his existence after death. These are ways in which they came to understand him from their experiences of him after the crucifixion.

Jesus is alive

Some texts are content to state the fact that Jesus is 'alive' (see Luke 24:5, 24:23, Acts 1:3, 25:19). We are reminded of Jesus' words to the Sadducees: 'God is God not of the dead but of the living; for to God all people are in fact alive' (Luke 20:37-38). This is beautifully expressed by Jesus at the Last Supper: 'I will not leave you orphans; I will come back to you. In a short time, the world will no longer see me; but you will see me, because I live, and you will live' (John 14:18-19). The world will not see him, because the seeing is not a matter of physical sight but of enlightenment. The seeing will be a seeing of the heart and mind illumined by faith: an experience had by those who could say with Paul: 'I live no longer I. It is Christ who lives in me' (Galatians 2:20).

Jesus is assumed into heaven (into the presence of God)

Certain exceptional people in the history of Israel were thought of as having been assumed into heaven: Enoch (Genesis 5:24), Moses (Deuteronomy 34:5-6) Elijah (2 Kings 2:11), Jeremiah (1 Maccabees 2:58), and others (Psalm 49:15). The New Testament writers use this same model to speak of Jesus (see Acts 1:2,9,11,22; Luke 9:51; Mark 16:19; 1 Timothy 3:16). The Beloved Disciple, as usual stressing Jesus' freedom, prefers a more active word. He speaks of Jesus 'going up' to heaven, rather than being 'taken up' (see John 1:51, 3:13, 6:62, 20:17).

The New Testament speaks of Jesus having been 'raised on high' (John 3:14, 8:28, 12:32, 12:34; Acts 2:33, 5:31; Philippians 2:9, Hebrews 7:26). These expressions assert, not only that Jesus is alive, but that he is with God.

Jesus is glorified

We speak of a glorious day when the beauty of the day (the trees, the flowers, the sky, the smiling people) is so radiantly manifest that we are moved to rejoice. The word is used frequently in the scriptures for the wonder, power, love and beauty of the Creator that is manifest in the events of this world and in nature. Isaiah was overwhelmed by the presence of God in the Temple. In his ecstasy, he saw two seraphs who 'cried out one to another in this way: holy, holy, holy is YHWH of hosts. His glory fills the whole earth' (Isaiah 6:3).

A favourite image for God's real but mysterious presence is that of the shekinah or 'glory-cloud'. The scriptures speak of the cloud covering the Temple, surrounding the people, and coming down on the mountain. It is a way of indicating God's mysterious presence. The idea is captured in the final words of the Book of Exodus: 'The cloud (glory-cloud) covered the Tent of Meeting and the glory of YHWH filled the tabernacle. Moses could not enter the Tent of Meeting because of the cloud that rested on it and because of the glory of God that filled the tabernacle. Whenever the cloud rose from the tabernacle the people of Israel would resume their march. If the cloud did not rise, they waited and did not march until it did. For the cloud of YHWH rested on the tabernacle by day, and a fire shone within the cloud by night, for all the House of Israel to see. And so it was for every stage of their journey' (Exodus 40:34-38).

Luke speaks of Mary being caught up in the cloud at the moment of Jesus' conception (Luke I:35). The disciples on the mountain of Transfiguration (Mark 9:7; Matthew 17:5; Luke 9:34) are in the cloud.

When people die and are buried, we can no longer see them. When Luke comes to speak of what happened to Jesus, he says 'a cloud took him from their sight' (Acts I:9). He is speaking of the glory-cloud. Jesus was caught up in the embrace of God. When God's majesty, power, love and beauty were revealed in the experiences of the early Christian community, it was Jesus whose presence was so powerfully manifested. It was radiantly obvious to them that it was the Spirit of Jesus that filled them. It was this Spirit that was powerfully drawing all people to Jesus, living now in the glory of God.

It seems that the concept of glory in relation to Jesus was first associated with the final manifestation of Jesus when history reaches its climax in the so-called Last Judgment. This was something to which the early community looked forward. They believed that Jesus was present in their midst. The glorious manifestation of his presence, however, was still to come. This seems to be the idea in Mark: 'Then they will see the Son of Man coming in the clouds with great power and glory; then too he will send the angels to gather his chosen from the four winds, from the ends of the world to the ends of heaven' (Mark 13:26-27; Mark 8:38). Matthew follows Mark in this (Matthew 16:27, 19:28, 24:30, 25:31), as does Luke (9:26, 21:27).

That Jesus is in the glory of God will be manifest when God's will triumphs and God's justice is seen to prevail. This is sometimes spoken of as the 'parousia' ('presence manifested'; see 2 Thessalonians 1:10; Titus 2:13; 1 Peter 4:13). The Beloved Disciple, reflecting back over the life of Jesus, sees the beginnings of this glory already present in the wonder of Jesus' person and actions. In his Prologue he writes: 'We saw his glory, the glory that is his as the only Son of the Father, full of grace and truth' (John 1:14). The first signs of this glory were seen in the life of Jesus (John 2:11; see 7:39), but the hour of his glorification, according to the Beloved Disciple, was the hour of his complete self-giving, and final life-giving: the hour of his crucifixion. Jesus, though dead, was alive, for from his pierced heart the life-giving Spirit poured forth (John 19:34).

This same idea seems to be in the mind of the Synoptics when they speak of the veil of the temple being torn at the moment of Jesus' death (Mark 15:37; Matthew 27:51; Luke 23:45). The veil was there to symbolise the inability of people to look on the face (the glory) of God. Now, at this supreme moment of Jesus' life, the veil is torn asunder. Now we can look on the face of Jesus and see there the glory of God (2 Corinthians 4:6).

Looking at the post-crucifixion experiences of the disciples, we find the New Testament writers speaking of Jesus as having entered his glory (Luke 24:26): 'He is the radiant light of God's glory and now he has gone to take his place in heaven' (Hebrews 1:3; also Hebrews 2:7,9). Paul uses the same imagery (Romans 6:4; Philippians 3:21; 2 Corinthians 4:4), as does Peter (1 Peter 1:21; see Acts 3:13).

To speak of Jesus being glorified is to speak of the wonder and praise that was aroused because of the liberation in people's lives through Jesus' action in the community of his disciples: action which radiantly manifested the healing and redeeming love of God.

Jesus is resurrected

In the Isaiah scroll, we find evidence for the belief that God would vindicate the just person (Isaiah 52:13-53:12), and in the Book of Wisdom (chapter 3) and in Daniel (chapter 7) we find evidence of the Greek concept of the immortality of the soul. However, it is only with the heroic self-sacrifice of the martyrs of the anti-Syrian war (168-165 BC) that we find explicit statements of a conviction that God would ultimately conquer even death and restore his faithful ones to life. As they buried their loved ones and knew that their bodies would lie corrupting in their graves, the people began to hope that on the day of God's judgment, these bodies would be restored to life, and that, in this way, their death would be vindicated. Not everyone thought in this way. Because the idea was not to be found in the ancient tradition, the Sadducees rejected it as heretical (see Acts 23:8).

The disciples of Jesus found in this expression the best way of declaring what had happened already to Jesus. Before analysing in detail what the New Testament has to say on this subject, let us be clear about what the documents are not saying. First, they are not asserting that the risen body is like the body we now know. Secondly, they are not asserting that the risen body is such as to be able to be seen with our physical eyes. We have already referred to the fact that Paul dismissed as being 'stupid' curious questions about the kind of body we have in the risen life (1 Corinthians 15:35). We think in images, and the only images we have of the human body are those drawn from our own experience. We cannot hope to imagine correctly the body that belongs to the life-beyond-death. This element of mystery permeates all the Gospel resurrection stories.

Likewise, the words translated 'see' in these same stories are not referring explicitly to physical sight. The most common word, Greek *horao*, derives from the same source as our word 'aware'. It can quite accurately be translated 'be aware of'. We find it being used of an evil spirit 'seeing' Jesus (Mark 9:20). Obviously, there is no implication that the spirit had an ocular sensation! We find it being used of 'seeing' God (Matthew 5:8). This is not to say that there was no ocular sensation involved in the resurrection appearances; though one may well wonder whether a physically blind disciple would have missed anything. What we are saying is that the 'seeing' is an enlightenment of the mind and heart, a 'seeing' that requires faith.

Mary Magdalene recognised Jesus not with her eyes but with her heart when he called her by name (John 20:16). The disciples on the road to Emmaus recognised Jesus not with their eyes (Luke 24:16) but in the breaking of bread (Luke 24:31). The 'eyes' that were opened were the 'eyes' of their minds, opened to understand the meaning of the scriptures (Luke 24:27, 32). The disciples by the lakeside clearly did not recognise the risen Jesus with their physical eyes (John 21:12). The word 'see' in relation to the risen Jesus stands for a perception of faith and love, a recognition by the heart, an awareness and conviction that flows from an insight born of revelation.

The appearance accounts are not presenting us with visual snap-shots, but with profound statements of faith-experience, told and re-told, because what happened to Mary and to Thomas and to the disciples by the lake, what happened to the community assembled at the Eucharist and at Pentecost, was typical of the experiences had by many people after Jesus' death.

There was something special about the 'seeing' of Jesus' disciples (John 20:29; 1 Peter I:8). Their seeing was a recognising, for, having seen Jesus prior to his death, they were able to recognise that the one they were experiencing in the period after the crucifixion was the same Jesus of Nazareth whom they had known. It was the crucified one who was now alive and active among them.

The word 'risen' translates two Greek words. The first is *'egeiro'*, which basically means to 'awaken', in the sense of gathering one's thoughts and feelings that have been scattered in sleep (Matthew 1:24, 2:13-14, 2:20-21, 8:25, 25:7, 26:46). *'egeiro'* is also used of a person who stirs themself to activity (Matthew 8:15, 8:26, 9:5-7, 9:19, 12:11, 17:7). On a number of occasions, it is used to convey the idea of a person being awakened from the sleep of death back to this life (Matthew 9:25, 10:8, 11:5, 14:2). It is not surprising then that the same imagery is used to give expression to the idea of being awakened from the sleep of death into the life-beyond-death with God. Matthew uses it in this sense of the 'resurrection' (Matthew 16:21, 17:9, 23; 20:19, 26:32, 27:52-53, 63-64). The idea being conveyed is that God wakened Jesus from the 'sleep' of death to a new life.

The second Greek verb *'anhistemi'* and the noun *'anastasis'* means to 'stand up'. In relation to Jesus, it is conveying the image of Jesus lying prostrate in the tomb, and then standing up to carry on his life and activity. Obviously, we are dealing with an image. What the resurrection concept adds to the concepts of life, exaltation and glorification, is the belief that the one who lives and is assumed into heaven and is in the glory of God is experiencing a full, though transformed, human life. Death has been conquered.

The disciples had distinct human, personal experiences. Certain definite things happened to them. We looked at some of these experiences in the first part of this chapter. The effect of these experiences, happening as they did to so many people in so many different ways, caused them to come to the realisation in faith (call it illumination, revelation, seeing) and the conviction that Jesus was alive and present in their lives and history. They articulated this belief in a number of symbolic images and expressed it in the appearance stories of the Gospels, particularly the Gospels of Luke and the Beloved Disciple. These, like the parallel stories of Paul's conversion in the Acts (9:1-27, 22:1-21, 26:9-23), express in story form the enlightenment they experienced and their conversion to faith in Jesus. He is alive. More than that, physical death has been shown not to have the last word. This was the ultimate proof of God's love and the ultimate source of their hope. If not even death can separate us from God's love, we have nothing to fear and are liberated to live in faith and hope and love.

III: The empty tomb

All four Gospels record the fact that some of the women went to the tomb on the first day of the week, only to find that the body of Jesus that had been buried there on the Friday evening was not there. Before looking at the material more closely, let us establish what the Gospels are not saying. It is obvious that the empty tomb is not presented as a proof of the resurrection. The resurrection cannot be proven in any scientifically satisfying way. It does not belong to the empirical order. What is evident is that the disciples, from being scattered, came back together again, and that they shared a conviction based on real, actual experiences. Their interpretation of their experiences cannot be refuted, nor can it be established. It is a faith-interpretation. It made sense to their minds, it convinced their hearts, and their lives are perhaps the best argument for their belief. We have already looked at some of the experiences on which their faith was based. It was not founded on the empty tomb. This is obvious from the texts themselves.

Mark concludes his account with the words: 'The women came out and ran away from the tomb because they were frightened out of their wits; and they said nothing to a soul, for they were afraid' (Mark 16:8). 'They said nothing to a soul'. The 'seeing' of Jesus was to take place in Galilee (Mark 16:7).

Matthew's account is basically the same as Mark's (Matthew 28:1-8) except that in Matthew: 'Filled with awe and great joy the women came quickly away from the tomb and ran to tell the disciples' (Matthew 28:8). As in Mark, the recognition was to take place in Galilee (Matthew 28:7; see 28:16-20).

Luke is even more explicit. When the women discover that the body of Jesus is not in the tomb 'they stood there not knowing what to think' (Luke 24:4), and when they told the apostles: 'this story of theirs seemed pure nonsense, and they did not believe them' (Luke 24:11).

The faith of the apostles in the resurrection is based on personal encounters with Jesus, not on anything as ambiguous as an empty tomb. In the Beloved Disciple's account, Mary concludes: 'They have taken the LORD out of the tomb and we don't know where they have put him' (John 20:2). Her conclusion turns out to be wrong, but only because of her encounter with Jesus, or rather his encounter with her. The only one portrayed as believing on discovering the empty tomb is the Beloved Disciple (John 20:8). In other words, the empty tomb can be a sign of the resurrection, but only to the eyes of one who loves.

This is the role of the empty tomb in Christian piety. The early Jerusalem community, and later pilgrims, came to the empty tomb. What more powerful symbol could there be to celebrate the power of God over death? Death was 'swallowed up in victory' (1 Corinthians 15:54). 'Death shall be no more' (Revelation 21:4-5). The empty tomb stood as a token of an already existing faith, already existing because of the confirmatory experiences had by those who followed Jesus. It is these experiences that gave meaning to the empty tomb. Mark's account seems to be saying this by the ordering of his words: 'He has risen (experiences), he is not here (in the empty tomb)' (Mark 16:6).

The Gospel accounts seem to present what was an early liturgical re-enacting of the community's faith. The pilgrims would come with their lighted candles to the tomb, and there celebrate, as we still do in our liturgy, their faith in the resurrection of Jesus. In typical Biblical style, the empty tomb is portrayed as a theophany. It is God who illumines their minds to understand the reason for the empty tomb: Jesus is risen. That Jesus is risen was discovered by the first disciples when they returned to Galilee: it is there that they 'saw' him. The pilgrims would have to discover him also in their own lives.

Writing for the frightened, persecuted community of Rome, Mark ends his Gospel with the promise 'they will see me in Galilee'. He is inviting the community to faith. Each person and each community has to go on with their life in trust. Moses had to journey into the unknown, sustained by God's promise to be with him; so also, disciples of Jesus must walk in faith, even through persecution. Only in the journey itself will we know the presence, the power and the peace of the risen Jesus, and of his Father in whose glory he is living.

Matthew adds that this meaning that the empty tomb came to have was itself a revelation of Jesus. He was present to the women even in the emptiness of the cemetery (Matthew 28:9-10). Jesus did indeed meet them in Galilee, on the mountain of prayer; for it was in Galilee that they re-grouped and became aware of Jesus commissioning them to 'Go, make disciples of all nations' (Matthew 28:19). In this mission, they were sustained by the promise 'Know that I am with you always; yes, to the end of time' (Matthew 28:20).

Conclusion

After his death, Jesus graced his disciples with certain privileged experiences of his presence and love. These experiences find expression in the Gospel portraits of Jesus' appearances. They also provide the meaning of the empty tomb. The appearances express the faith; the empty tomb symbolises it. The faith is not based on the portraits; they are based on the faith. The faith is grounded in personal, intimate, experiences had by Jesus' disciples.

The 'resurrection of Jesus' is the most compelling and satisfactory way of speaking of Jesus being with God and with his disciples, for it speaks of the transformation of his human nature by God. It is, however, only that: a way of speaking, an imperfect model. That Jesus is alive is absolutely central to Christianity. It is central because it is the ground of our conviction that the good news is true. God was indeed faithful and loving to Jesus; so we can trust that God will be so to us as well. Life is meaningful, even in the face of death. It was for Jesus; we can hope it will be for us. Our experience of the life of God has a special Jesus-quality about it now. It is the living Jesus who calls us to follow him, invites us into prayer-intimacy with him, inspires us to love as he loves, and enables us to do so by his present love flooding our hearts. We are able to call

God 'Abba', because we are brothers and sisters of Jesus. He is praying for us now in the presence of his Father (Romans 8:34, Hebrews 7:25). He is sending us now on a mission of love to the whole of creation, to convince the world that it is loved and that therefore it can love. There is no need now for sin, or distraction, or the dissipation of energy in anger, frustration and violence. Peace is possible.

All of this, in fact the whole of the Christian faith and way of living, rests on the wonder, joy and astonishment of the good news that the crucified one is indeed risen and alive and with us on our journey till the end of time.

This means that, while we expend our energy in trying to bring about the reign of God's love here on earth, at the same time we recognise that for us, as for Jesus, our hope is not limited by death. Death is the horizon beyond which we cannot see, but it is not the end of life. The threat of death cannot reduce us to impotence, any more than it deflected Jesus from his path. There is no question of taking our eyes away from this world in which we live. We are to live here and now, and this life is the only one we are equipped to live.

There is no escape from it, nor can an other-worldly piety substitute for giving our lives to bring about the reign of God 'on earth as in heaven' (Matthew 6:10). But while we give all our hearts and minds and strength to the healing and strengthening of the human condition, we are freed from measuring everything within the horizons of birth and death. Jesus' resurrection opens up eternal possibilities. The goal of all our activity is fullness of life beyond death.

Moreover, we ought not deny or ignore the kind of mystical experience that Saul of Tarsus had on the road to Damascus, to which generation after generation of Christians have since witnessed. Of course, we can deceive ourselves, and we can be deceived; we can misinterpret and misunderstand. But false mysticism does not rule out authentic mysticism. And if Jesus is alive in God, why could he not do what many a saint has claimed he has done, and choose, love, trust and commission us to be his disciples? Paul could write: 'I live now not with my own life but with the life of Christ who lives in me' (Galatians 2:20).

Belief in the resurrection of Jesus is basic to Christianity. Paul wrote: 'If Christ has not been raised then our preaching is useless, and your believing it is useless' (1 Corinthians 15:14). The resurrection gives us an ultimate perspective on suffering and death and is the ground of our belief in the fidelity of God. Freed from the fear of death we are free to live.

Sharing in Jesus' Eternal Communion with God

We are graced now to 'become participants of the divine nature' (2 Peter 1:4), sharing Jesus' Spirit, his intimate communion with God. In the First Letter of John, we are assured: 'Beloved, we are God's children now; what we will be has not yet been revealed. What we do know is this: when he is revealed, we will be like him, for we will see him as he is' (1 John 3:2).

The Book of Revelation offers us the following symbolic portrait of the Risen Jesus in glory:

> I turned to see the voice that was speaking to me,
> and on turning I saw seven golden lamp stands,
> and in the midst of the lamp stands
> I saw one like the Son of Man clothed with a long robe
> and with a golden sash across his chest.
> his head and his hair were white as white wool,

white as snow;
his eyes were like a flame of fire,
his feet were like brass, refined as in a furnace,
and his voice was like the sound of many waters
In his right hand he held seven stars, and
from his mouth came a sharp, two-edged sword
and his face was like the sun shining
with full splendour. (Revelation 1:12-16).

The Gospel of the Beloved Disciple includes Jesus' prayer: 'Father, I desire that those also, whom you have given me, may be with me where I am, to see my glory, which you have given me because you loved me before the foundation of the world' (John 17:24).

The author of the Letter to the Hebrews assures us the glorified Jesus is praying for us: 'He is able for all time to save those who approach God through him, since he always lives to make intercession for them' (Hebrews 7:24, 25). 'Christ entered into heaven itself, now to appear in the presence of God on our behalf' (Hebrews 9:24).

CHAPTER TWELVE

JESUS THE SAVIOUR OF THE WORLD

The God of Israel redeemed the Israelites from Egypt: 'I am the LORD, there is no other saviour but me' (Isaiah 43:11). Jesus' disciples came to recognise Jesus as the presence of God completing God's redemptive and saving action in their lives. Jesus' name means 'the LORD is salvation' (see Matthew 1:21). His coming was greeted by Mary, his mother, with the cry 'My spirit exults in God my Saviour' (Luke 1:47), and by Zechariah: 'Blessed be the LORD, the God of Israel, for he has visited his people, he has come to their rescue and he has raised up for us a power for salvation' (Luke 1:68). Simeon, an old man who longed for the fulfilment of God's promises, held the child Jesus in his arms and prayed: 'Now, Master, you can let your servant go in peace, just as you promised; because my eyes have seen the salvation which you have prepared for all the nations to see, a light to enlighten the pagans and the glory of your people Israel' (Luke 2:29-32).

John the Baptist is portrayed as preparing the way for Jesus, in whom 'all people will see the salvation of God' (Luke 3:6, quoting Isaiah 40:5). In previous chapters, we have seen that Jesus was understood to be Immanuel, the one in whom God was present to his disciples, the temple of

God's abiding presence among them, the one in whom they experienced the Holy Spirit of the life-giving and redeeming God. Jesus was the one who expressed in the human condition (in the 'flesh') God's word to them. Jesus was God's Wisdom and God's focal Word. In this chapter, we will concentrate on the redemption and salvation which Jesus' disciples experienced. In the light of Jesus' resurrection, we know that Jesus' saving presence and action continues in our lives today.

Jesus redeemed people, and so they came to experience freedom. Jesus saved them, and so they came to experience meaning, direction and hope in their lives. In Jesus, they believed that their God brought about a new Exodus, a new Passover; he brought them into a new communion through a new covenant and a new way. Moreover, the history of the early Christian communities brought Jesus' disciples to the realisation that what Jesus had done for them had significance, not only for them, but for the whole world.

Jesus gave his message, his 'good news' in word; he also, and more significantly, gave it in the way he lived, the choices he made, and the values he espoused for which he gave his life. It was a message of love, a convincing message because he was acutely aware of what was inhibiting love in his world, and he accurately, courageously and unrelentingly worked against all that was keeping the people bound, and leading them away from belief in the living God, and so from belief in themselves and in their world. Jesus continues his mission today.

The main thing reducing Jesus' contemporaries to despair was their understanding of evil and its power over their lives. They lived in fear of the demonic. Jesus declared that evil had no power over him (John 14:30), and that the power of evil had been condemned (John 16:11) and overthrown (John 12:31). In his sermon at the house of Cornelius, Peter states: 'God had anointed Jesus with the Holy Spirit and with power, and because God was with him, he went about doing good and curing all who had fallen into the power of the devil' (Acts 10:37-38; see also 1 John 3:8). The world into which Christianity spread after Jesus' death seems to have been even more dominated by this fear. Many thought of themselves as caught in the grip of fate and imprisoned in a meaningless world. Paul assured them that they had been liberated from 'this present wicked world' (Galatians 1:4), and from the 'power of darkness' (Colossians 1:13).

Again and again in the Gospels, Jesus is presented as light overcoming darkness, as good overpowering evil, as the one who is filled with the Holy Spirit and who casts out any evil spirit. The first miracle of Jesus recorded by the Synoptics, in which a man suffering from convulsions is healed by Jesus' teaching (Mark 1:29-39), is portrayed in this way, as is the account of the paralysed man who is released from his sin (Mark 2:1-17), and the epileptic boy (Mark 9:14-29). Jesus' ministry is presented as putting to flight everything that is a threat to life: 'I have come that they may live and live to the full' (John 10:10).

The extent of God's power, realised in the ministry of Jesus, is portrayed in three successive scenes. We looked at them in Chapter Nine. Together they illustrate Paul's statement that 'Nothing can ever come between us and the love of God made visible in Christ Jesus our LORD' (Romans 8:39).

The first scene is the storm on the lake (Mark 4:35-4; Matthew 8:23-27; Luke 8:22-25). It powerfully portrays Jesus who showed, again and again throughout his life, that nothing that happens around a person, nothing that threatens a person from outside, can take away the protection and love of

God. That he believed this himself is clear from the way he approached his own death.

The second scene takes us to the pagan land on the opposite shore, the land of the Gadarenes (Mark 5:1-20; Matthew 8:28-34; Luke 8:26-39). It is one thing to have a storm raging around us; it is another to have a storm raging within. Living among the tombs on the hillside is a man possessed. He is a symbol of someone with a psyche broken by the ravages of a dislocated world. Jesus liberates him from the 'legion' of forces that warred within his psyche. In Jesus' presence he found healing and peace.

In the third scene the reign of God's love penetrates even beyond the veil of death, as Jesus takes a little girl by the hand and restores her to life (Mark 5:21-43; Matthew 9:18-26; Luke 8:40-56). Death was thought to be the result of sin and to express the ultimate power of evil, since it wrenched people away from life, and therefore, as it was thought, from union with God. Jesus 'set free all those who had been held in slavery all their lives by the fear of death' (Hebrews 2:15). Ultimately it was by the way he approached his own death, by his peaceful and prayerful acceptance of it, and by the fact that he remained confident in the power of his Father's love to 'save him out of death' (Hebrews 5:7), that he gave death a new meaning and robbed it of its 'sting' (1 Corinthians 15:55).

The liberation effected by Jesus was not automatic. The Hebrews did not have to leave Egypt, and they are frequently represented as longing to go back. The journey across the desert seemed too demanding. It was the same for Jesus' contemporaries. They did not have to be liberated, and they could go back to the 'security' of the Law and the temple and the ways of life to which they had grown accustomed. But Jesus, like Moses before him, was there to lead them across the desert, and to stay with them till they reached the Promised Land. He asked them to place their trust in God as he did, to accept the challenge he gave them, and to journey with him along the way. This point is portrayed dramatically when, after the three powerful scenes just described, Jesus comes to his hometown. We are told: 'He could work no miracle there. He was amazed at their lack of faith' (Mark 6:5-6).

Jesus placed his trust in his Father's love. He asks the same trust of us. He manifested the presence of God's love. He asked people to *'be-lieve'* in it (to *be* in this *love*), to open their hearts to receive it, and to allow it to work miracles in their lives. Love does not force itself. The all-powerful love of God can liberate us only if we welcome it.

Other factors inhibiting faith – factors related to the contemporary fear of the demonic – were their false images of God. Jesus' contemporaries understood suffering as the result of God's rejection of the sufferer. The scene with the leper (Mark 1:40-45) is a perfect example of this. The leper was ostracised, and in God's name (see Leviticus 13). Jesus, in the name of the living God, embraced him. Likewise, with the man born blind (John 9:1-41). Jesus' acceptance of his own suffering forced people to see suffering's relationship to God's will in a different, and liberating, light. There is also their understanding of riches as a proof of God's blessing. The rich young man was of this mind, as were Jesus' own disciples (Mark 10:17-31). Jesus' words and life challenged them to question their assumptions and offered them a way out of finding their value in possessions. 'No one's life is made secure by what they own, even when they have more than they need' (Luke 12:15).

Jesus also liberated people from traditions that claimed to be religious, and from laws that claimed to define God and express God's will, but which were, in fact, causes of oppression:

'How ingeniously you get round the commandment of God in order to preserve your own tradition' (Mark 7:9). 'Alas for you lawyers, because you load on people burdens that are unendurable, burdens that you yourselves do not move a finger to lift' (Luke 11:46). The Sadducees and the Pharisees are portrayed as authorities that upheld such false gods. We see Jesus' attitude forcefully expressed when he does not fast (Mark 2:18-22) and when he takes a walk on the Sabbath, and when he heals a man with a withered hand (Mark 2:23-3:6). The fig tree that was all show, full of leaves but with no fruit, was a symbol of the kind of institutionalised religious practice that failed to assuage people's hunger for God (Mark 11:12-14). The temple that Jesus emptied was a symbol of the same, for it failed to help people find communion with God; it failed to be a house of prayer, and it was not 'for all the peoples' (Mark 11:15-19).

Jesus liberated people from the useless spiral of violence engaged in by the Zealots who saw warfare as an instrument of God's will. Jesus told the people to 'love your enemies and pray for those who persecute you' (Matthew 5:44). We are told: 'As he drew near and came in sight of the city, Jesus shed tears over it and said: If you, in your turn, had only understood on this day the message of peace' (Luke 19:41-42). His own behaviour confirmed his teaching: 'Father, forgive them; they do not know what they are doing' (Luke 23:34). He liberated them also, if they wanted such liberation, from distrust of people. He ate with the outcasts of society (Matthew 9:41), and commissioned his disciples: 'Go, make disciples of all the nations' (Matthew 28:19). We are all children of the one Father whose saving and liberating love is for all.

The New Testament uses a number of images to portray Jesus as redeemer and saviour. One is that of 'leader' (Greek:

archegos). 'As it was his purpose to bring a great many of his children into glory, it was appropriate that God should make perfect through suffering the leader who would take them to their salvation' (Hebrews 2:10). God is our *'arche'*, the source and origin and goal of our existence. Jesus is our *archegos*, our way to the Father (John 14:4-6). Like Moses, he walks with us through the desert: 'With so many witnesses in a great cloud on every side of us, we too should throw off everything that hinders us, especially the sin that clings so easily, and keep running steadily in the race we have started. Let us not lose sight of Jesus, who leads us in our faith and brings it to perfection. For the sake of the joy which was still in the future, he endured the cross, disregarding the shamefulness of it, and from now on has taken his place at the right hand of God's throne' (Hebrews 12:1-2). Peter speaks of Jesus as the one who leads us to life (Acts 3:15), as the one whom God raised up to be our 'leader and saviour' (Acts 5:31), as our 'chief shepherd' (1 Peter 5:4).

Linked with the image of leader is that of 'brother'. Jesus, our redeemer, is one of us, one 'from among yourselves, from your own brothers' (Deuteronomy 18:15). 'The one who sanctifies, and the ones who are sanctified, are of the same stock; that is why he openly calls them brothers. It was essential that he should become completely like his brothers (Hebrews 2:11, 17; see Mark 3:35; Matthew 25:40, 28:10; John 20:17; Romans 8:29). Jesus not only shows us the way to live, he walks the way with us, and since he is completely like us, since he is 'as all people are' (Philippians 2:7), he enables and encourages others to walk with him.

A third image, linked to that of leader, is that of a 'shepherd' who goes out in search of the straying, wounded and lost sheep (Matthew 18:12-14). Paul tells us that Jesus 'came into the world to save sinners' (1 Timothy 1:15) and Jesus himself said: 'The Son of Man has come to seek out and save what is lost' (Luke 19: 10; see Mark 6:34; Matthew 9:36). He is spoken of as one who, like David, will 'shepherd my people Israel' (Matthew 2:6, quoting Micah 5:1); and as one who, like Moses, is the 'great shepherd of the sheep' (Hebrews 13:20, quoting Isaiah 63:11). Peter speaks of Jesus as the 'guardian and shepherd of your souls' (1 Peter 2:25; see 1 Peter 4:5). The Book of Revelation recognises him as shepherd over all the nations (Revelation 2:27, 12:5, 19:15). Jesus is the 'good shepherd who lays down his life for his sheep' (John 10:11). He is the shepherd who is struck down in death (Mark 14:27; Matthew 26:31), who seals with his blood an eternal covenant with God (Hebrews 13:20). He leads us, as a shepherd, to 'springs of living water' (Revelation 7:17). He is the shepherd who 'sacrificed himself for us in order to set us free' (Titus 2: 14). 'Remember the ransom paid to free you from the useless way of life your ancestors handed down was paid in the precious blood of Christ' (1 Peter 1:18)

It is 'through his blood' that we 'gain our freedom' (Ephesians 1:7; see Colossians 1:14). To speak of Jesus as the redeemer-shepherd is to associate him with the Exodus journey, and so with another image, that of the Passover Lamb. The Beloved Disciple speaks of him as the 'Lamb of God that takes away the sin of the world' (John 1:29 and 1:36). It is this imagery that pervades the Last Supper account and the Passion. It is also a favourite image in the Book of Revelation where it occurs twenty-eight times. There the exalted Jesus is spoken of as the Lamb who was sacrificed (Revelation 5:12), as the Lamb who is victorious (Revelation 7:10), as the Lamb who 'will lead them to springs of living water' (Revelation 7:17), as the Lamb who invites everyone to the marriage feast (Revelation 19:9), as the Lamb who is a lamp in the temple of the city of God (Revelation 21:23).

Jesus liberates people that we might experience greater and greater freedom to live life to the full (see John 10:10). 'Where the Spirit of the LORD is, there is freedom', wrote Paul (2 Corinthians 3:17). 'When Christ freed us, he meant us to remain free' (Galatians 5:1). The Beloved Disciple has Jesus say: 'If you make my word your home you will indeed be my disciples, you will learn the truth and the truth will make you free. If the Son makes you free, you will be free indeed' (John 8:31-32, 36).

Jesus frees people 'so that they could be his very own and would have no ambition except to do good' (Titus 2:14, quoting Exodus 19:5). Jesus continues to free us. Jesus frees us so that we can 'discover the will of God and know what is good, what it is that God wants, what is the perfect thing to do' (Romans 12:2). Jesus frees us so that we can fill our minds with 'everything that is true, everything that is noble, everything that is good and pure, everything that we love and honour, and everything that can be thought virtuous or worthy of praise' (Philippians 4:8). Jesus frees us so that we will 'resist evil and conquer it with good' (Romans 12:21). Paul writes, 'Try to imitate God, as children that God loves, and follow Christ by loving as he loved you, giving himself up in our place as a fragrant offering and sacrifice to God' (Ephesians 5:1-2). Like Jesus, the disciple who has been liberated is to give their life to bring about the 'new heavens and new earth, the place where righteousness will be at home' (2 Peter 3:13). Redemption is in view of salvation – a life lived according to God's purpose and in communion with God.

Jesus' own salvation came finally only when he was redeemed from death by his Father. Jesus enjoys fullness of life in the exaltation of heaven. It will be the same for us. 'Our homeland is in heaven' (Philippians 3:20). We are still 'waiting for our bodies to be set free' (Romans 8:23; see Ephesians 4:30). 'We must be content to hope that we shall be saved –our salvation is not in sight, we should not be hoping for it if it were – but, as I say, we must hope to be saved since we are not saved yet – it is something we must wait for with patience' (Romans 8:24-25).

It is possible to be 'sure of the end to which your faith looks forward' (1 Peter 1:9). The New Testament is full of statements of the experiences of Jesus' disciples – experiences that gave them this assurance: 'When we were reconciled to God by the death of his Son, we were still enemies; now that we have been reconciled, surely we may count on being saved by the life of his Son? Not merely because we have been reconciled, but because we are filled with joyful trust in God, through our LORD Jesus Christ, through whom we have already gained our reconciliation' (Romans 5:10-11; see 2 Corinthians 5:18-19).

This joyful trust is based primarily on our experience of Jesus' Spirit in our lives. 'Remember it is God himself who assures us all, and you, of our standing in Christ, and has anointed us, marking us with his seal and giving us the pledge, the Spirit that we carry in our hearts' (2 Corinthians 1:21-22). Moved by this Spirit, we, like Jesus, call God 'Abba' (Romans 8:15, Galatians 4:6). Jesus has taught us to look on God as a Father whose love is faithful and constant. The good news leads to a life of 'righteousness and peace and joy brought by the Holy Spirit' (Romans 14:17).

Paul prayed for the community in Rome: 'May the God of hope bring you such joy and peace in your faith that the power of the Holy Spirit will remove all bounds to hope' (Romans 15:13). Peter, too, wrote to those who were following

Jesus: 'You are already filled with a joy so glorious that it cannot be described, because you believe; and you are sure of the end to which your faith looks forward, the salvation of your souls' (1 Peter 1:8). In his Letter to the Romans, Paul wrote: 'Through our LORD Jesus Christ by faith, we are judged righteous and at peace with God, since it is by faith and through Jesus that we have entered this state of grace in which we can boast about looking forward to God's glory' (Romans 5:1-2).

Paul recognised that he and his community were constantly graced by God. He invites them to remain open to that gracious love, upheld by their knowledge that Jesus remained convinced even on the cross that his Father's unconditional love would remain with him and redeem him from death. Their experience of the Spirit of Jesus among them was such as to 'remove all bounds to hope' (Romans 15:13). It is the same for us.

Jesus is frequently called 'saviour' (see, for example, Luke 2:3; Acts 5:31, 13:23; 1 Timothy 1:1, Titus 1:4, Titus 3:6; 2 Peter 1:1, 3:18; 1 John 4:14). In Jesus, his disciples experienced God giving meaning and direction to their lives. It was Jesus who brought them into intimate communion with the Father. Peter claimed that Jesus was 'the only one by whom we can be saved' (Acts 4:12). In a Letter composed within the community of the Beloved Disciple, we read: 'anyone who has the Son has life; anyone who does not have the Son does not have life' (1 John 5:12). Paul claimed that Jesus was the 'yes' to all the promises made by God (see 2 Corinthians 1:20).

This was the experience of Jesus' disciples. It was also the experience of those who, throughout the Roman Empire, came to know Jesus through the Christian community. Paul observed that both Jew and Gentile had found communion with God 'by being redeemed in Christ Jesus' (Romans 3:24).

Jesus was the answer to the hopes and dreams of Israel. He was also the answer to the hopes and dreams of the nations. Paul noted this in his letter to the Colossians: 'The good news which has reached you is spreading all over the world and producing the same results as it has among you ever since the day when you heard about God's grace and understood what this really is' (Colossians 1:6). So it is that we read: 'The living God is the Saviour of the whole human race' (1 Timothy 4:10). 'God's grace has been revealed, and it has made salvation possible for the whole human race' (Titus 2:11).

The Gospel of the Beloved Disciple expresses the same insight. The Samaritans declare: 'We know that he really is the saviour of the world' (John 4:42; see 1 John 4:14). Jesus himself declares: 'I am the light of the world. Anyone who follows me will not be walking in the dark; they will have the light of life' (John 8:12; see John 9:5). After the Sanhedrin had decided to kill Jesus, we hear: 'Jesus was to die for the nation – and not for the nation only, but to gather together into unity the scattered children of God' (John 11:51-52). The authorities complained: 'The whole world is running after him' (John 12:19). Some Greeks at the festival asked to see Jesus (John 12:21) and Jesus' words in response to this request are: 'When I am lifted up from the earth, I shall draw everyone to myself' (John 12:32). 'He is the sacrifice that takes our sins away, and not only ours, but the sins of the whole world' (I John 2:1-2).

Our search for meaning, for salvation, is in reality a search for love, and a search for love that goes beyond all the limits of this finite world. Our search is a religious one, a longing for a love that is unconditional and unrestricted. This is the kind of love Jesus gave. When he loved them, his disciples believed that his love was the love of God. Jesus' love engaged their religious experience, drew them into the mystery, and invited them into communion with God. When Jesus liberated them, they experienced it as a liberation brought about by God. They found themselves able to call God 'Abba', as Jesus did. Jesus put words to God's Word and gave a face to God's Glory. They came to recognise him as the one through whom God was communicating with them in human terms. Surrounded by Jesus' love, they came to realise that Love was the real name for what they had, till then, called God.

No doubt their insight into the meaning of Jesus came only gradually, and deepened throughout the years he was with them, and then throughout the years after Jesus' death when they experienced his presence among them. Their thoughts kept coming back to the cross. In that hour of darkness, when the pain, and frustration, and sin and anger of his enemies fell upon him and tried to crush him – it was then that he showed who God really is, by the manner in which he kept believing and kept loving, and what we, as human beings, are capable of when we believe in God's power to save. In the light reflected from the cross, everything else Jesus said and did became a sign of God's redeeming and saving love. To contemplate Jesus pierced on the cross (John 19:37) is to see unrestricted, unconditional love – a love offered to every human being. Anyone who wants may 'draw water joyfully from the springs of salvation' (Isaiah 12:3). Anyone who believes can find meaning there for their life, healing, and direction. We can find there the communion with God that our hearts desire. The language of the cross is, indeed, 'God's power to save' (1 Corinthians 1:18).

Jesus' disciples invite each of us to join Thomas in recognising in Jesus 'my LORD and my God' (John 20:28), and, knowing we are loved, to grow into the fullness of life for which we are made and for which we long.

CHAPTER THIRTEEN

SO, WHO IS JESUS?

This book has been about Jesus, a carpenter from Nazareth, known as the son of Joseph (John 1:45) and Mary (Mark 6:3), the friend of Peter, James, John and the other disciples. His life is recorded in the Gospels. He is the person about whom Paul preached. The Christian community over the centuries has looked to him as the revelation of God.

We have been looking at him, not only as the object of people's love, gratitude, admiration and faith, but also as the subject of relationships with other people and with God. He is the one who asked Andrew and another disciple of the Baptist to come and see where he lived. He is the one who spoke the beatitudes, who wept over the city he loved, who dreamed and hoped, and who suffered and gave his life for his friends. He is the one who prayed to God as 'Abba'.

Jesus' humanity

Jesus of Nazareth is a man. At first glance, this seems so obvious that one might wonder what is the point of stating it. However, the history of Christianity shows that it was Jesus' humanity that was the first thing to be denied. Ignatius of Antioch at the end of the first century, Justin of Flavea Neapolis a little later, and the Council of Chalcedon in the middle of the fifth century, all found it necessary to proclaim this simple and obvious truth against those who denied that Jesus was truly human, denied that he was 'like us in every respect' (Hebrews 2:17), 'except sin' (Hebrews 4:15).

Even today there are those who, while giving lip service to the reality of Jesus' humanity, continue to portray Jesus in such a way that we find it impossible to identify with him. It is as though people today like to portray Jesus with all the beauty we can create, so long as we do not have to face up to the often harsh and quite demanding reality of his actual historical existence, with all that it implies for us about our aims, decisions, choices, life-style and commitment to God, to humanity and to the world.

Whatever else needs to be stated in answer to the question 'Who is Jesus?', it must never deny or alter the simple and obvious truth that he is a man. Jesus is not some kind of half-man, half-god. He is not a super-man. He does not have a unique humanity that puts him in a species all on his own. His body was a human body, just like ours; his psyche was a human psyche, just like ours. His feelings were human; his thoughts were human; his way of understanding was human; his way of coming to clarity, of pondering, deciding, and responding, was human, just like ours.

He did not have some secret source of information that enabled him to bypass the ordinary processes we have to go through in our search for understanding. When we watch him, we are watching one man's way of being a human being. No two people are the same. True, we all share what we term 'human nature' – which is another way of speaking of the limits within which we have to live our life – but we do it in uniquely personal ways. We may not be able to do everything Jesus did, because we are who we are, and he is Jesus; but we are not to look for an explanation of the uniqueness of his humanity in some extra, mysterious reality that is outside our experience. His insights, his religious experience, his decisions, his courage, and his heroically faithful love, as well as his hope and his faith, were all human qualities of this remarkable person.

Jesus was human like us. Therefore, he had to live within the limits of human nature. However, the way he lived demonstrates the error of many cherished assumptions about what those limits are. According to those who were closest to him, Jesus did not sin. This truth opens up amazing possibilities for us all and demonstrates what human freedom can achieve when a person responds as beautifully as did Jesus to the call arising from his religious experience. We must take seriously the fact that Jesus, human like us, was capable of such self-giving and such freedom and such love, for it opens up undreamed of possibilities for us all. We must take seriously also his faith, for it was his faith that was the spring from which everything else flowed. The secret of Jesus' personality is to be found in his intimate religious experience.

God is not an object of human perception. God is not an object for us. God was not an object for Jesus. Jesus' human religious experience was of the same nature as yours and mine. That is to say, he experienced himself as being loved unconditionally and without reserve by the one we call God, and he called, more personally, 'Abba'.

In our day, as in the days of Jesus, some people attempt to define God in ways that fit in with our distractions, or provide an object for our fears, or satisfy our fancy, or justify our power. Jesus accused many of his contemporaries of idolatry, as did the prophets before him, and we, today, are surrounded by idolatry. False gods flourish in our churches and in our minds and hearts. Particularly in recent years, reaction against idolatry has led many people into atheism or agnosticism. God is placed in the too hard, or the irrelevant, basket. This frees us from the mess into which idolatry gets us, and it appears to leave us in control of our own destiny. We are tempted to accept as true only what we can be sure of from the point of view we have adopted. The problem, however, is that this ignores the whole area of human experience that we call religious.

Or we can, like Jesus, take our religious experience seriously, and set out on a journey of discovery, responding in faith, in hope, and in love, to the mysterious Presence that is at the heart of our being loved. This does not lift us onto another plane. It does not remove the mystery and the harsh realities of suffering and death and sin, but it does shed light on the human condition, and the fruit of genuine religion can be discerned by anyone who cares to look.

When Jesus responded to the Sacred Mystery at the heart of his own existence, he responded with the word 'Abba'. Abba is a human word, arising in the human psyche of Jesus. Its explanation, like the explanation for everything else Jesus said and did, must be sought in his human experience. As the New Testament testifies, it is possible for others to share in the intimacy that Jesus experienced. We too can call God 'Abba' as we experience the Spirit of God's love flooding our hearts. It was Jesus of Nazareth who awakened us to the marvels that were going on in our lives – marvels we had failed to observe, or in which we did not dare believe.

The results of his response to God are recorded in the Gospels. Problems did not disappear; people still managed to resist his overtures and his challenge. He was murdered by those who considered themselves the official custodians of truth and especially of the truth concerning God. But Jesus continued to believe; he continued to hope; and he continued to love, right up to his death. However unique and beautiful,

Jesus' religious experience was human, and it must be understood as such. To do otherwise is to distort the picture given us in the New Testament.

Jesus' divinity

Christians believe that Jesus of Nazareth, the same Jesus about whom we have said he is human, is also divine. This has been the constant belief of the faithful, expressed in our liturgical worship, in which we associate Jesus with our worship of God. We looked at what it means to speak of Jesus as divine in Chapter One.

When Jesus speaks of God, he is speaking of his experience of being unconditionally loved. The Beloved Disciple expresses this beautifully in his Prologue: 'No one has ever seen God. It is the only Son, who is in the bosom of the Father, who has made God known' (John 1:18). Jesus puts it this way: 'The Father knows me, and I know the Father ... The Father loves me' (John 10:15, 17).

The Beloved Disciple in his Gospel constantly focuses on Jesus' communion with God: 'The one who comes from heaven (from communion with God in prayer) testifies to what he has seen and heard' (John 3:31-32). 'The one who is from God has seen the Father' (John 6:46). Jesus experienced himself as on a mission given him by God: 'The living Father has sent me, and I live because of the Father' (John 6:57). 'I know the Father because I am from the Father and it is the Father who sent me' (John 7:29).

Jesus' words flow from his communion with God. 'He whom God has sent speaks God's words, for he gives the Spirit without measure' (John 3:34). 'My teaching is not mine but the Father's who sent me. Anyone who resolves to do the will of

God will know whether the teaching is from God or whether I am speaking on my own' (John 7:16-17). 'I declare to the world what I have learned from God ... I speak these things as the Father instructed me' (John 8:26, 28). 'I declare what I have seen in my Father's presence' (John 8:38). 'I know God, and I keep God's word' (John 8:55). Do you not believe that I am in the Father and the Father is in me? The words I say to you I do not speak as from myself' (John 14:10). 'The word that you hear is not mine. It is from the Father who sent me' (John 14:24). In a prayer to God, Jesus says: 'The words that you gave me I have given to them, and they have received them and know in truth that I came from you; and they have believed that you sent me' (John 17:8).

As early as the end of the first century, Ignatius of Antioch included Jesus when he spoke of God. He was giving expression to the faith of the Church, a faith expressed in the Gospel of the Beloved Disciple in which Thomas experiences the presence of God in the Risen Jesus and exclaims 'My LORD and my God' (John 20:28).

Jesus' divinity is his intimate communion with God, a divinity that he invites us to share.

Jesus' self-knowledge

When Jesus thought about himself, he reflected with a mind like ours. When he asked the question 'Who am I?', what insights did he have? What conclusions did he draw? We are not speaking of Jesus' consciousness here. We are exploring his self-knowledge. Bernard Lonergan SJ clarifies the distinction: "What is conscious is experienced. But human knowing is not just experiencing. Human knowing includes experiencing, but adds to it attention, scrutiny, inquiry, insight, conception, naming, reflecting, checking, judging' (*The response of the Jesuit as priest and apostle in the modern world*, in *A Second Collection*. London, Darton, Longman and Todd, 1974, page 172)

An obvious place to go to find an answer to our question about Jesus' self-knowledge is the New Testament; more precisely, the Gospels. However, there are certain critical questions that need to be answered before we can simply accept every word that is placed on Jesus' lips as direct evidence of his personal psychic awareness. If Jesus had written the Gospels, we could rightly see in them direct evidence of his thoughts on many matters, including himself. But he didn't write the Gospels, his disciples did. If we could establish that Jesus actually spoke the words attributed to him and were sure of the context and the manner of his speaking, then we could use these words as data, and by assuming reasonable psychic consistency, we could deduce much about his own self-image and self-understanding. However, while we can reach a high degree of probability concerning certain sayings of Jesus, and while we can be confident that the gist of his words and their overall direction are not at variance with Jesus' own intentions, aims and character, we must accept that the Gospels bring us, in the first instance, into contact with the way Jesus was understood by their authors and by those who accepted the Gospels as authentic. Sometimes the context may have more to do with the questions and experience of the Christian community at the time than with that of Jesus himself.

I say this not to suggest that the picture we have of Jesus in the Gospels may not be accurate – the whole of this book insists that it is. I say it only to alert the reader to the truth that it is one thing to know on the word of the Beloved Disciple that Jesus is indeed the 'light of the world' (John 8:12). It is another thing to suggest that that is the way Jesus saw himself.

If the words can be shown to be those of Jesus, we have our answer. If, on the other hand, they are the Beloved Disciple's words, placed on the lips of Jesus to express the reality and so the truth, but without claiming to express also Jesus' own psychic awareness of the truth, then we ought not jump to the conclusion that the Gospels gives us evidence in regard to Jesus' psyche. Because the gospels are human documents, we can expect to find in them some evidence to help us answer our question, so long as we remember that the Gospels were not designed to explore Jesus' psyche. We must be careful in our critical analysis of the texts.

Only when we can establish that Jesus actually spoke certain words can we use them as evidence in an argument concerning his self-understanding. At the same time, since the Gospels are true to who he was and to his aims and mind and attitudes, we can be a lot more confident in the sayings than was once thought. If the Beloved Disciple had wanted to make the claim that Jesus was the light of the world, he could easily have done so. The fact that he chose to have Jesus himself make that claim is at least an indication, not only of its truth, but also of the fact that he considered it to be part of Jesus' own self-understanding as well.

There is ample evidence that Jesus realised the special nature of the intimacy he experienced in his relations with the God whom he called 'Abba'; a realisation he expressed in speaking of himself as the Son of God. In Chapter One, we noted that nowhere in the Gospels is Jesus portrayed as claiming to be God. When he is accused of doing so, he defends himself against the accusation by proclaiming his total dependence on the Father. He is God's Son, not to be identified with the Father. However, we do find him claiming an authority that is divine, and in an unprecedented way.

Those who knew and loved Jesus came to the conclusion that in getting to know Jesus they were getting to know God. They based this conclusion on their experience of Jesus, including post-crucifixion experiences, which were, of course, not part of the data that Jesus could reflect upon prior to his death. But when Jesus saw how people responded to him with a religious response, he must surely have reflected on the meaning of this for himself.

Any conclusions that Jesus reached concerning his relationship to his Father did not free him from having to live in the ambiguities of the human condition. Far from lifting him above faith, or removing him from wonder, they must have heightened for him the mystery of his human existence. If Jesus' disciples had to live with the profound mystery of their relationship with Jesus, and the recognition that it was God who was being revealed to them in Jesus, imagine what it must have been for Jesus to live with this same mystery in the depths of his own psyche. Imagine how he must have pondered its implications for his living and his dying and his mission. This did not short-circuit the journey of Jesus as he came to terms with his growing recognition of who he was in his relations with others and especially in the intimacy of his prayer with the one he called "Abba".

Doctrine of the Trinity

Coming to know the God Jesus called 'Father', and coming to know Jesus as God's Son, and coming to experience the divine life-giving Spirit, Jesus' disciples came to speak of God as Father, Son and Holy Spirit. When the authors of the New Testament use this language, they are referring to God, Jesus, and the intimate communion between God and Jesus.

When Christianity moved from the Semitic to the Greco-Roman world, people attempted to achieve a more abstract clarity in which to express their belief. Over the centuries, theologians found various Greek words that were useful as tools of expression of the Church's belief concerning Jesus and his relationship with God: words like *ousia, hypostasis, physis* and *prosopon*. None of these words could hold the mystery, and each of them had to be understood as carrying a new weight of meaning. Believing Christians, enlightened by their faith-experience, could be protected by these definitions from going up the dead-ends that were declared heresies. Keeping faithful to the creeds, they could be led into prayer, and into their profound encounter with God: Father, Son and Holy Spirit.

Without a full comprehension of what is essentially mysterious, people came to think of God as communion in love. While we cannot comprehend this, we can have some inkling of it from our own experience of the intimacy of love and communion between lovers. Truth about any person can be attained only by one who loves that person. Truth about Jesus can be attained only by one who is committed to the journey of discipleship and who has experienced redemption and salvation in the community that is committed to him. It can be attained only by reflection on personal and communal Christian religious experience.

Conclusion

The effect of the various creedal statements is to demand that we take Jesus seriously, recognising the reality of his human experience, human consciousness and human commitment, as well as recognising that it is this human life that is our most precious revelation of God and, in human terms, a coherent and trustworthy statement of the way God has chosen to reveal God's Self to us.

All our ideas about God must be checked against the actual attitudes of Jesus of Nazareth. All our understanding of God's revelation, through all the experiences of humanity and the many sacred books that are cherished by us, including the sacred books of Jesus' own people (the Bible) – all these have to be checked against the words spoken by Jesus as interpreted by his contemporaries and expressed in the New Testament, and as interpreted by the community of Jesus' disciples in the changing circumstances of history since.

Before the time of Jesus, people could look at nature, and look at history and infer certain things from them about God. They could point to the Exodus event and say, 'that is what God has done!', and so 'that is what God is like!'. People could reflect on their own religious experience, they could listen to the prophets; they could examine the Torah and come to know about God. Jesus' disciples learned to point to Jesus and say 'That is what God has done! That is what God is like!' Jesus, whose human existence we can see, reveals to us in a human way the character, the will and the being of God.

The next step

Our investigations have attempted to find in the New Testament answers to the question 'Who is Jesus?' Enlightened by the answers, our next task is to investigate what meaning Jesus might have for us and for our world.

We find the following scene in Luke's history of the early Christian community in Jerusalem:

> Once, when Peter and John were going up to the
> Temple for the prayers at the ninth hour, it happened

that there was a man being carried past. He was a cripple from birth; and they used to put him down every day near the Temple entrance called the Beautiful Gate so that he could beg from the people going in. When this man saw Peter and John on their way into the Temple, he begged from them. Both Peter and John looked straight at him and said, "Look at us". He turned to them expectantly, hoping to get something from them, but Peter said, "I have neither silver nor gold, but I will give you what I have: in the name of Jesus the Nazarene, walk!" Peter then took him by the hand and helped him to stand up. Instantly his feet and ankles became firm, he jumped up, stood, and began to walk, and he went with them into the Temple, walking and jumping and praising God. Everyone could see him walking and praising God, and they recognised him as the one who used to sit begging at the Beautiful Gate of the Temple. They were all astonished and were unable to explain what had happened to him. (Acts 3:1-10)

Challenged by the religious authorities, Peter made the claim that Jesus was the only one who could save not only the crippled man but us all (see Acts 4:12). Whatever the forces crippling us 'we should throw off everything that hinders us, especially the sin that clings so easily, and keep running steadily in the race we have started. Let us not lose sight of Jesus' (Hebrews 12:1-2).

The history of the Christian Church has been a story of a struggle between fidelity and infidelity: fidelity to genuine religious experience and to a humble and courageous living out of the community's vision and values, inspired by the memory and the presence of Jesus; and infidelity, with the intrusions and distortions that have occurred when those who claim to follow Jesus lose sight of him.

Our aim in this book has been to clarify who the real Jesus of Nazareth is, so that, whatever the forces crippling us, we will not lose sight of him. Our next task is to name what it is that is crippling us, in the way Jesus named the oppressions that were crippling his contemporaries. In this book we have not attempted to do this, except in passing. It is a task that must be attempted. Without some knowledge of the real Jesus, we would not have the courage to do so, for a Jesus that is unrelated to history, to reason and to any real world, a Jesus that is not really concerned with bringing about God's will on earth, cannot give us the energy to face our real situation. Only the real Jesus can remove false religion that keeps us spiritually numb and encourage us to believe that we can 'get up and walk'.

Jesus, whom we have attempted to discover in this book, lived in a real world, and was concerned with real people. He named and vigorously opposed anything that made it difficult for people to live. In so doing, he incurred the opposition of many people; hence his death. But he also won the confidence of the oppressed. They trusted him, and so learned to trust God, and to believe in themselves, in their world and their future. This was because Jesus revealed the powerful love of the redeemer God.

Keeping our eyes on Jesus, let us dare to face and name today's oppressions. As we seek to understand what it is that is crippling us, let us learn from Jesus to believe that God is really drawing everyone. Let us recognise the fact that everyone has a sacred religious experience that must be respected. Let us reject anything sectarian and trust our own and other people's personal religious experience. On this basis alone can we hope to find the peace that Jesus offers, and release on earth the healing and redeeming love of God.

Our world is desperately crippled, desperately hungry for meaning, and thirsty for love. Too much idolatry, too much false religion, too many false Jesus, have added to the confusion and driven too many honest people into a lifeless agnosticism. Those of us who claim to follow Jesus have an obligation to our world to ensure that when we present Jesus as the answer to our modern ills, it is the real Jesus of Nazareth that we present. He is the revelation of the one and only God. He is the 'only one by whom we can be saved' (Acts 4:12).

www.ingramcontent.com/pod-product-compliance
Lightning Source LLC
Chambersburg PA
CBHW010245010526
44107CB00063B/2687